Routine Politics and Violence in Argentina

Close to three hundred stores and supermarkets were looted during week-long food riots in Argentina in December 2001. Thirty-four people were reported dead, and hundreds were injured. Among the looting crowds, activists from the Peronist Party (the main political party in the country) were quite prominent. During the lootings, police officers were conspicuously absent – particularly when small stores were sacked. Through a combination of archival research, statistical analysis, and multisited fieldwork and drawing on the perspective of contentious politics, this book provides the first available analytic description of the origins, course, meanings, and outcomes of the December 2001 wave of lootings in Argentina. It scrutinizes the gray zone where the actions and networks of both party activists and law enforcement officials meet and mesh. The book also makes a case for the study of the gray zone in less spectacular, but equally relevant, forms of political activity. Clandestine connections between established political actors, this book argues, count in the making of collective violence and in routine political life.

Javier Auyero is an associate professor of sociology at the State University of New York, Stony Brook. He was awarded a John Simon Guggenheim Fellowship in 2001 and a Harry Frank Guggenheim Fellowship in 2005. He is the author of *Poor People's Politics* and *Contentious Lives* and has published articles in *Theory and Society, Ethnography, Mobilization, Latin American Research Review*, and *Journal of Latin American Studies*, among others.

Cambridge Studies in Contentious Politics

Editors

Jack A. Goldstone   *George Mason University*
Doug McAdam   *Stanford University and Center for Advanced Study in the Behavioral Sciences*
Sidney Tarrow   *Cornell University*
Charles Tilly   *Columbia University*
Elisabeth J. Wood   *Yale University*

Ronald Aminzade et al., *Silence and Voice in the Study of Contentious Politics*

Clifford Bob, *The Marketing of Rebellion: Insurgents, Media, and International Activism*

Charles Brockett, *Political Movements and Violence in Central America*

Gerald F. Davis, Doug McAdam, W. Richard Scott, and Mayer N. Zald, *Social Movements and Organization Theory*

Jack A. Goldstone, editor, *States, Parties, and Social Movements*

Doug McAdam, Sidney Tarrow, and Charles Tilly, *Dynamics of Contention*

Kevin J. O'Brien and Lianjiang Li, *Rightful Resistance in Rural China*

Sidney Tarrow, *The New Transnational Activism*

Charles Tilly, *The Politics of Collective Violence*

Charles Tilly, *Contention and Democracy in Europe, 1650–2000*

Deborah Yashar, *Contesting Citizenship in Latin America: The Rise of Indigenous Movements and the Postliberal Challenge*

Routine Politics and Violence in Argentina

THE GRAY ZONE OF STATE POWER

JAVIER AUYERO

*State University of New York,
Stony Brook*

CAMBRIDGE
UNIVERSITY PRESS

CAMBRIDGE UNIVERSITY PRESS
Cambridge, New York, Melbourne, Madrid, Cape Town, Singapore, São Paulo

Cambridge University Press
32 Avenue of the Americas, New York, NY 10013-2473, USA

www.cambridge.org
Information on this title: www.cambridge.org/9780521872362

First published 2007

Printed in the United States of America

A catalog record for this publication is available from the British Library.

Library of Congress Cataloging in Publication Data

Auyero, Javier.
Routine politics and violence in Argentina : the gray zone of state power / Javier Auyero.
  p.   cm. – (Cambridge studies in contentious politics)
Includes bibliographical references and index.
ISBN: 978-0-521-87236-2 (hardback)
ISBN: 978-0-521-69411-7 (pbk.)
1. Food riots – Argentina.   2. Pillage – Argentina.   3. Violence – Argentina.
4. Political violence – Argentina.   5. Partido Peronista (Argentina).   6. Peronism.
7. Law enforcement – Argentina.   I. Title.   II. Series.
HV6485.A7A94   2007
982.07 – dc22   2006030228

ISBN   978-0-521-87236-2 hardback
ISBN   978-0-521-69411-7 paperback

For Esteban, reader of all books, source of all important ideas.
And for Tuki, who knows what really matters.

Contents

List of Figures, Maps, and Tables

Preface and Acknowledgments

> One might legitimately ask how, from my considerable distance in place and time from the events I am describing, I can know all that I claim to be a part of my brother's story.... And the answer, of course, is that I do not, in the conventional sense, know many of these things. I am not making them up, however. I am imagining them. Memory, intuition, interrogation and reflection have given me a vision, and it is this vision that I am telling here.
>
> Russell Banks, *Affliction*, p. 47

> There is not one simple, "animal," response to hunger.... "Riot" ... is not a "natural" or "obvious" response to hunger but a sophisticated pattern of collective behaviour, a collective alternative to individualistic and familial strategies of survival. Of course hunger rioters were hungry, but hunger does not dictate that they must riot nor does it determine riot's forms.
>
> E. P. Thompson, *Customs in Common*, p. 266

In 1989, when the first food riots in modern Argentine history occurred, I was living in Buenos Aires – close, in fact, to one of the epicenters of the violence. Years later, in December 2001, when the episodes this book describes and seeks to understand took place, I was not in Argentina. I watched brief images of the sacking of food markets and other stores on TV and read about them on-line in the Argentine newspapers. At the time, I thought we were witnessing pretty much the same thing as in 1989: people were hungry, they couldn't take "it" anymore, and they exploded – in 1989, "it" was soaring prices in the midst of a hyperinflationary peak; in 2001, "it" was a combination of an inept government and a dramatic economic crisis. Collective suffering, I thought then, couldn't go on much longer without manifesting itself in some dramatic way. Chaotic and desperate lootings were the result of many – too many and too fast – being pushed against the ropes. While watching the 2001 episodes on TV and reading about them in the newspaper, I also recalled the human toll of the 1989 lootings and began wondering what would happen this time, when events were apparently more massive: How long would it take for the government and its repressive apparatus to control the mayhem? How many would be dead and injured (and soon forgotten)? How terrible would the human and material devastation be when things calmed down? At the time, the lootings received some media attention, but the events in the main plaza and the streets of Buenos Aires captured the spotlight: The *cacerolazos* (as the banging of the pots and pans in protest against government policies came to be known), the brutal repression that left thirty-five dead (and no one punished), and the political crisis that ended the De La Rua government and put the Peronist Party back in office became the main story.

The 2001 lootings lasted about a week; things eventually calmed down and, while the study of popular protest in Argentina became a sort of mini-industry among scholars and activists interested in Latin American politics, the food riots quickly retreated into oblivion – explained away as a collective but disorganized response to hunger, pretty much along the lines of my own thinking at the time. This book recovers the lootings from that oblivion and seeks to reconstruct what happened during those episodes by focusing on their dynamics and meanings.

Why scrutinize the lootings? Who cares about them many years afterward? As the reader will soon realize, in and of themselves, the lootings are interesting, multifaceted episodes. And, as we will see, people (participants, bystanders, victims, public officials, and grassroots leaders) care deeply about them. Truth be told, I was extremely surprised when top public officials made room in their busy schedules on short notice to talk about events that happened years ago. I was even more surprised at the vehemence that officials and grassroots leaders put into their accounts ("I am so angry about what happened. Anything you need, please do not hesitate to contact me again," a prominent activist told me; "anything you need...I also want to know what happened," a top official confessed). Shopkeepers and residents also took time to talk to us and to dwell on the many details of those days as if they were reliving them right then and there. But the main reason for attempting the reconstruction of the lootings is twofold: The food riots are a unique window into contemporary Argentine popular politics and a wonderful opportunity to extend our knowledge of the political dynamics of collective violence. If we know which questions to ask them, then the story the lootings tell exceeds the actual events and speaks of issues, I will argue, to which students of politics around the world should be paying closer attention.

Carried out from a "considerable distance in place and time," this reconstruction is based on old-fashioned fieldwork and archival research, and it is informed by an ethnographic sensibility that keeps vigilance over a scholastic view all too common among those who study the relationship between collective suffering and popular contention. Fieldwork in different communities and in the archives gave me a vision of what happened from December 14 to 22, 2001, of how politics tends to work in modern Argentina, and of the dynamics and meanings of collective violence. This book tells of this vision.

Many, many people helped me in the creation of this vision. First and foremost, I want to thank the residents and shopkeepers in La Matanza and Moreno for trusting me with their stories about events that, mainly in the case of the victims of violence, shook their lives. I am also extremely grateful to Vanesa da Silva and Graciela Rodriguez, my two hard-working research assistants on this project. They helped me locate the fieldwork sites, conducted many interviews, and shared with me their own views of the events. Rodrigo Hobert, fellow sociologist and unwavering entertainer, helped me in the creation of the catalog of the events.

This book draws on my own fieldwork and that of others. For sharing their field notes with me and for enriching dialogues, I'm thankful to Marina Sitrin, Karina Mallamacci, and Magdalena Tosoni. In Buenos Aires, Horacio Verbitsky proved to be not only an intelligent interlocutor with whom I discussed the main thrust of this book but also a source of crucial contacts that, literally, changed the course of my inquiry. Eduardo Cura facilitated my access to the archives of Channel Eleven, where Osvaldo Petrozzino kindly showed me images of the lootings – some of them never broadcast before. Thanks to all.

Mia Bloom, Elizabeth Borland, Mona El-Ghobashy, Daniel Fridman, Leslie Gates, Michael Hanagan, James Jasper, Jackie Klopp, John Krinsky, Roy Licklider, Francesca Polletta, Sherrill Stroschein, and Sidney Tarrow provided comments on two earlier drafts of the Introduction and Chapter 4 during two lively sessions at the Columbia Contentious Politics Seminar. I also presented a draft of the same chapter at the Economic Sociology Workshop at Princeton University; many thanks to Patricia Fernandez-Kelly and Viviana Zelizer for a constructive session. When I thought the book was "almost done," I took it on a tour to California to test how it fared. Nina Eliasoph, Paul Lichterman, and Pierrette Hongdaneu-Sotelo at the University of Southern California and Beatriz Sarlo, then visiting at UC-Berkeley, may not know it but I found enough encouragement in their comments to push me deeper into this project. I then realized that the book was not "almost" but only "half" done and that I needed to further conceptually dissect and empirically explore the notion of gray zone. I then took another tour with the book "half cooked," this time to the South, to Argentina, where I shared many of the ideas and empirical findings with researchers and colleagues at a meeting organized by Valeria Brusco from Centro de Estudios en Política y Sociedad (CEPYS)–Córdoba. Part of a series called *In Vino Veritas*, the discussion that followed my rather disorganized presentation helped me to refine some of my arguments. Thanks to Valeria and her colleagues for their interest, comments, and, of course, the wine. I'm also grateful to my colleagues at the Centro de Estudios en Cultura y Política (CECYP), with whom, surprisingly after all these years, we keep editing the journal *Apuntes*, particularly Marina Farinetti and (again) Daniel Fridman (whose comments I heeded carefully), and my dear friend Lucas Rubinich (again, Lucas, *gracias*). An early version of the Introduction and of Chapter 4 was presented at the *Seminario Internacional: Ciudadanía, sociedad civil y participación política* organized at the University of Buenos Aires on September 1–2, 2005, and then published in the *Journal of Latin American Studies*. Thanks to the many participants who heard and provided encouragement and criticism; to Isidoro Cheresky, who organized a wonderful two-day seminar; and to the editor of *JLAS*, James Dunkerley, for his encouragement. I also want to thank Gastón Beltrán, John Markoff, and my colleagues at Stony Brook,

Preface and Acknowledgments

Michael Schwartz, Naomi Rosenthal, Andrea Tyree, and Ian Roxborough, who made trenchant criticisms and suggestions on earlier drafts. Timothy Moran, colleague and skilled statistician, helped me to create a statistical model of the looting dynamics out of data I collected from newspaper sources. A snapshot of our joint work is reproduced here in the Appendix (an extended version was published in the journal *Social Forces*). I am also indebted to my graduate students, past and present members of the Ethnography Workshop at Stony Brook. The new generation of Stony Brook ethnographers had to put up with me while I was writing this book. Unbeknownst to them, I tested some of the ideas during the ethnography seminar I taught in the spring of 2005. Thanks then to Diana Baldermann, Larissa Buchholz, Lauren Joseph, Carol Lindquist, Matthew Mahler, Etsuoko Marouka-Ng, Tyson Smith, and Amy Traver for being patient with me while I was thinking out loud and for being wonderful sources of ideas, energy, and fun. Carol, editor extraordinaire, carefully cleaned this manuscript from weird, incorrect, or all-but-*Spanglish* expressions while challenging me to go further into my understanding of the relationships between the gray zone and democracy. Thanks to Jessica Giovachino whose architectural skills were put to good use in the making of Figure 5.

I am very grateful to the staff at the Laboratorio de Sistemas de Información Geográfica from the Instituto del Conurbano at the Universidad de General Sarmiento who were diligent in making the maps presented here. Without the generous funding provided by the Harry Frank Guggenheim Foundation and without a sabbatical leave made available by my home institution, Stony Brook University, I would not have found the time to conduct the research – much less to transcribe, analyze, and write up the results.

I've done this twice already, and I need to do it a third time. This whole business of writing books began when, I still don't know whether intentionally or not, my former advisor Chuck Tilly referred to my then-dissertation as a book. Since then, I've been thinking in terms of books – both reading them and writing them. Chuck was the first to read the research project that started all this, and he made critical comments along the way. He then read the final version and provided his by-now legendary insights – both substantive and stylistic. As the reader will see, much of the argument of this book is a critical dialogue with Tilly's work. *Muchas gracias*, Chuck. I am also very grateful to my editor at Cambridge, Lew Bateman; to the Contentious Politics Series editor, Jack Goldstone; and to two anonymous reviewers. It is not exaggeration to say that their careful reading and astute criticisms and suggestions made a crucial difference in the final product.

Summers in the United States are a good time to do fieldwork in Argentina. I had, and still have after so many years, the same ambiguous feelings about that time. On one hand, I spend time doing what I like most about this craft, talking with people, listening to them, engaging with them. I also spend time with my friends down in Argentina. During the course of this project, Esteban and Shila, Tuki and Valeria, were there to ... well, they know. When I was too tired after long days in the field, they took me on a two-day trip to Mendoza that merits a book all on its own. On the other hand, summers are time away from *mi tribu*, the loved ones up here. Gabriela, *compañera*, Camilo and Luis, *amigos mios*, I promise I will make up for the time lost.

Introduction

Snapshots of Collective Violence

- Dozens of middle-aged men and women, youngsters and children, are gathered in front of a small supermarket somewhere in the province of Buenos Aires. It's hot. Many men have naked torsos, most are wearing shorts. The store's metal gates are broken, and people are holding them up so that others can enter. People are moving in and out of the store quite fast, but not rushing. They look cautious, but not afraid. They come out of the store with their hands full of goods, as much as they can hold. The voice of the reporter says, "*Saqueos en el Gran Buenos Aires* (Lootings in Greater Buenos Aires)."
- Hundreds of people are gathered in front of El Chivo, a supermarket in the district of Moreno, in the province of Buenos Aires. Most are on foot, some walk around with their bicycles. Some have placed their looted goods on the ground, apparently waiting for others who are still in the store – which can be seen in the background. A group of youngsters put a couple of bottles of beer in a box and chat, seemingly trading goods. Suddenly, everybody begins to run away. Some use the supermarket carts to carry their recently obtained items.
- It's night. The blinds of a butcher shop are torn apart; youngsters are coming out with large cuts of meat. Sirens can be heard in the background. Suddenly the police arrive on the scene. One cop tells people inside the store to leave. People start running out of the store. Those holding pieces of meat are stopped by another police agent; they abandon the meat cuts on the floor and keep running.

1

Figure 1. Lootings in Conurbano, December 19, 2001.

Figure 2. Lootings in Conurbano, December 19, 2001.

Figure 3. Lootings in Conurbano, December 19, 2001.

Figure 4. Lootings in Conurbano, December 19, 2001.

- A woman from the poor barrio La Travesía in the western part of the city of Rosario tells the camera: "We were told that we were going to receive bags of food, and we didn't get anything. They (the police) started shooting. We are here to ask for food, only a little bit of food, we are not asking for more." The police begin to shoot at the crowd. Most people run away, while others throw rocks at the police.

- A reporter informs the public that in the southern part of the Conurbano Bonaerense,[1] protesters are heading toward a large supermarket and demanding twenty kilograms of food. According to one protester, the managers are offering only "five hundred grams of flour for each family." After "moments of tension," municipal officials assure protesters that food will be distributed and the money for their unemployment subsidies (known then as *Planes Trabajar*) will soon be available.

- In most of these scenes, people are quiet. They do not hide themselves from the cameras – which in many cases are there before the police arrive. They go inside the stores, get as many goods as they can and walk away. Occasionally, however, they speak to the cameras. They speak about hunger but also about shame. Some of them scream at the cameras, others cry. "What did you get?" asks a reporter. "Everything," a man replies, with a somber smile. "And are you satisfied (*Y está conforme*)?" the reporter inquires. The man, not showing any surprise with such a ludicrous question, answers: "To tell you the truth, yes... because we are dying of hunger (*Porque nos estamos recagando del hambre*)." He leaves the scene walking, while the rest of the human traffic is orderly going in the opposite direction, seemingly on their way to get hold of their own share. "I am 30 years old. Can you imagine how ashamed my father is (*la vergüenza de mi papá*) as he watches me doing this?" a woman cries in front of the camera. Another one shouts: "We are hungry! Where's the mayor? I am alone, I have four kids; no one lends me a hand." A third, also crying, pleads: "There's a lot of hunger... there're no jobs. I

---

[1] The Conurbano is the metropolitan area adjacent to the capital city. It comprises thirty municipal districts.

have eight children; my husband is sick, I don't have enough to survive."[2]

These are quite varied snapshots of a series of events that Argentines still remember well: the December 2001 lootings. Some of the images are heartbreaking: desperate people asking "simply for a bag of food"; store owners frantically crying, unable to speak, while looters calmly carry goods out of their stores. Other images are familiar to, at least, Latin American eyes: police shooting rubber bullets and tear gas at crowds. In displaying collective violence by crowds against (sometimes) unprotected stores, the images invite viewers to take moral positions: Even if looters are "truly hungry," are they doing the right thing? Do store owners deserve this? The images call for morality; they also hint at relationality. They all show us different kinds of interactions: among looters; between looters and the looted, between looters and the police; between looters, store owners, and local officials. An understanding of all these interactions, however, is not to be found within them. We need to move outside of them, so to speak, to get a better grasp of what is going on and why the violence unfolds in the way it does. Once we do so, we begin to unearth some other (less visible) kinds of interaction – between, say, some organizers among the crowds and some police agents, between some store owners and some police agents, and so on – that were crucial during these episodes. By taking heed of the perspective of contentious politics, this book will take us as close as possible to where the truth of all these (hidden and overt) interactions lies. *Clandestine, concealed connections were central in making the lootings.* In the pages that follow, I focus much of my attention on these usually understudied relationships. These clandestine relationships constitute the gray zone of politics. Empirical and theoretical attention to this area is crucial, I argue in this book, to understand both routine and extraordinary forms of popular politics.

"We invite you to destroy the Kin supermarket this coming Wednesday at 11:30 A.M., the Valencia supermarket at 1:30 P.M., and the Chivo supermarket at 5 P.M." This and similar flyers circulated throughout poor

---

[2] These six brief stories were re-created on the basis of material taken from the visual archives of Channel Eleven and from the video *El Estallido*, produced by the newspaper *Página12*.

neighborhoods in Moreno, a district located in the west of the Conurbano Bonaerense, inviting residents to join the crowds that looted several dozen supermarkets and grocery stores on December 18 and 19. Investigative journalists' reports agree that the flyers were distributed by members of the Peronist Party, some of them local officials, others well-known grassroots leaders. The flyers betray a connection that analysts of the recent wave of violent contention in Argentina have consistently overlooked: the obscure (and obscured) links that looters maintain with established power-holders. The flyers, furthermore, point to a dimension that scholars of collective violence throughout the world have only recently begun to give due attention: the role of political entrepreneurs in the promotion, inhibition, and/or channeling of physical damage to objects and persons. By dissecting the specific actions of political brokers and the specific networks that they mobilized during the lootings of December 2001, this book sheds light on the intersection and interaction between routine politics and popular violence.

Neither the Kin, Valencia, and Chivo supermarkets nor most of the approximately three hundred stores looted throughout Argentina during the week-long wave of collective violence belong to supermarket chains. The largest chain supermarkets (known in Argentina as *hipermercados*) were, in fact, conspicuously absent from the list of stores ransacked by what mainstream newspapers described as "angry and hungry crowds." Several reports concur that the state police and the National Guard took special care when it came to protecting stores like the French-owned Carrefour and Auchan or the American-owned Norte while creating what grassroots activists called a "liberated zone" around small and medium-size stores – allowing political brokers and crowds to move freely from one target to the next. The spatial organization of repressive activities is indeed another key factor in the looting dynamics of that December. Together with an examination of the role played by party activists, the second empirical objective of this book concerns the form and the impact that the geography of policing had on the actual viability and variability of looting activity as well as on the amount of physical damage that was inflicted on stores and persons during the December 2001 episodes.

This book offers the first available analytic description of the lootings of December 2001. The research on which this description is based was guided by a series of theoretical concerns regarding the existing continuities between everyday life, routine politics, and extraordinary massive actions. It was through an interest in the relational character of collective violence that I engaged in this project.[3] This book, however, is not only concerned with the food riots. Throughout the text, I will divert attention away from the lootings, branching out from that main empirical focus, in order to show that the kinds of continuities and relations present in these episodes of collective violence also exist in other – less spectacular – forms of political activity. Thus, this book is as much about the mutual imbrication between politics and violence in contemporary Argentina as it is about these specific lootings.

Before I move into a brief revision of the diverse strands of scholarship on which I draw in my analysis, let me clarify, in telegraphic form, the main substantive and analytical messages of the book in order to provide a handy blueprint for the reader. In terms of the book's substantive claims: I argue that *clandestine connections count* in the making of collective violence and in routine political life. This book explores the available empirical evidence and unearths a set of concealed connections between established actors (political brokers, repressive forces, etc.) that shape the distribution and form of collective violence. It also offers several examples of the operation of clandestine connections in everyday, ordinary, politics. In terms of the book's analytical claims: I argue that political analysis should start paying *rigorous empirical attention to this gray zone* of semisecret political interactions.

Episodic Collective Violence in the Literature

The main focus of this book is on collective violence, here understood as "episodic social interaction that immediately inflicts physical damage on

---

[3] My objective was the refinement of existing theory (Snow, Morrill, and Anderson 2003) or, in Burawoy's (1998) terms the "restructuring of theory" of collective violence along the lines suggested by scholars who study the roles that violent entrepreneurs and police agents play in the unfolding of transgressive contention (Tilly 2003). I did not follow an "inductivist" or "grounded theory" approach. Data collection in this sense should be properly termed data production in that it is intimately bound with the theoretical construction of the object (Bourdieu, Chamboderon, and Passeron 1991; Wacquant 2002).

persons and/or objects ('damage' includes forcible seizure of persons or objects over restraint or resistance), involves at least two perpetrators of damage, [and] results at least in part from coordination among persons who perform the damaging acts" (Tilly 2003:3). Thus, this book will concentrate neither empirical nor analytical attention on everyday violence (Scheper-Hughes 1992; Bourgois 2001), symbolic violence (Bourdieu 1997; 2001; Bourdieu and Wacquant 1992), and/or structural violence (Farmer 2004; Wacquant 2004).

Explosions of Collective Violence in the North

Extraordinary outbursts of collective violence are hardly a monopoly of underdeveloped countries such as Argentina. During the last two decades, episodes of public unrest, in the form of massive lootings and riots, had also shocked advanced societies. Although a detailed review of each instance of urban disorder is beyond the scope of this book, I would like to briefly describe some of them and then concentrate some attention on one of the most recent episodes (the post-Katrina lootings). Despite dissimilar causes and forms, collective violence in the aftermath of a "natural" disaster shares common themes with the Argentine events under investigation here.[4]

Most North American readers are familiar with the explosion of civil violence that shocked Los Angeles in April 1992 following the acquittal of the four white police officers who were videotaped beating a defenseless Rodney King. Rioting and looting quickly spread outside the ghetto of South Central. Three days of violence left 2,400 injured and approximately 10,000 under arrest. The total damage was estimated at one billion dollars. As we will see in the next section, much of what we know about riot dynamics comes from social science research on these (and their 1960s' counterparts) episodes.

Most English readers will likely come up with other recollections of collective violence: the several nights in Brixton during April 1981, when youth riots left more than 300 injured, 83 buildings and 23 vehicles

---

[4] On the extent to which Katrina can be seen as an "unnatural" disaster, see the excellent collection of articles published on the Social Science Research Council Web site, especially Cutter (2006), Fussell (2006), Jackson (2006), and Smith (2006).

damaged (episodes were followed by other riots in London and Liverpool during July of that same year), or the events in Bristol during July 1992 when hundreds of youths rampaged through a local shopping center after two local men riding a stolen police motorcycle were killed in a collision with an unmarked police car (episodes were followed by similar ones in Conventry, Manchester, Salford, Blackburn, and Birmingham during that summer).

Analysts agreed that these urban disorders combined the logics of "bread" and "race" riots – protests against racial injustice and against economic deprivation and social inequality. Sufferers – mainly the youth of poor, segregated, and often dilapidated urban neighborhoods – deployed "the most effective, if not the only, weapon at their disposal, namely direct forcible disruption of civil life" (Wacquant 1993:5).

This double logic is also true for the most recent episodes of explosive collective violence in the First World, namely the November 2005 riots in France. Soon after teenagers Zyed Benna and Bouna Taore were electrocuted after climbing into an electrical sub-station in the Paris suburb of Clichy-sous-Bois (according to locals, they were hiding from the police), riots quickly spread through France. With youths burning cars and attacking public buildings and private businesses, violence multiplied in the suburbs of Paris and throughout "more than 270 towns" (*Guardian*, November 7, 2005) in the east (Dijon), north (Lille and Rennes), and south (Toulouse and Nice) of France, mostly geographically and socially circumscribed to the destitute neighborhoods of the suburbs known as "cités" or "quartier difficiles" (Roy 2006). Youngsters were again the main actors of the episodes, their manifest rage springing from "lifetimes of rampant unemployment, school failure, police harassment, and everyday racist discrimination" (Silverstein and Tetreault 2006:2). As of November 17, the violence resulted in "almost 9,000 torched vehicles and nearly 3000 arrests in nearly 100 municipalities across France" (Silverstein and Tetreault 2006:2).

Several commentators (Cesari 2006; Silverstein and Tetreault 2006; and Roy 2006) agree that the November riots were not isolated episodes.[5]

---

[5] See Silverstein and Tetreault (2006) for a summary description of episodes of violent popular unrest in France since 1980. On the recurrent character of French riots since

In point of fact, they are part of a long cycle of violent popular unrest that began in the early 1980s. As Kastoryano succinctly puts it (2006:1):

> Nothing is new with the last riots in France, they just lasted longer. . . . Ever since the 1980s, the press has been reporting the increasingly numerous riots in the French banlieues: among the most famous, Minguettes in 1981 and 1983, and Vaulx-en-Velin (both suburbs of Lyon) in 1990. These reports went along with pictures of burned-out cars, looted display windows, riots police, and young people throwing stones.

The point should be clear by now: Explosive collective violence, in the form of riots and lootings, is hardly a remnant of the past but part and parcel of life in contemporary societies of the advanced north – intricately tied to the very ways in which class, race, and ethnic inequities are structured and reproduced over time.

Contemporary First and Third World societies also witness the eruption of explosive collective violence in the immediate aftermath of "natural" disasters – usually in the form of food looting. This was the case after the flooding that devastated the state of Vargas in Venezuela in 1999, after the earthquake that shook the city of Armenia in Colombia that same year, and during the recurrent droughts that affect the Brazilian northeast. This was also the case in the first days after Hurricane Katrina struck New Orleans on August 29, 2005.

Although clearly "blown out of proportion" (Solnit 2005), looting "began at the moment the storm passed over New Orleans, and it ranged from base thievery to foraging for the necessities of life" (*New York Times*, September 29, 2005) – or what Christian Parenti calls "survival looting" (Parenti 2005). In the first days after the hurricane, dozens of drug stores, convenience stores, supermarkets, shoe stores, gas stations, electronics shops, auto parts stores, and gun and ammunition shops were ransacked (*Times Picayune*, September 1, 2005b; *New York Times*, September 29, 2005).[6]

---

the 1980s, see Roy (2006). For the different factors involved in the making of the November episodes, see Wieviorka (2006).

[6] The overwhelming majority (178 out of 223) of the suspects locked up in the temporary jail built in the New Orleans bus terminal ("Camp Greyhound") were accused of looting – most of them from Jefferson Parish (*Times Picayune*, September 9, 2005).

Introduction

According to several reports published at the time of the events, these lootings had some degree of internal organization and were facilitated by police inaction and/or complicity. During the events, existing reports agree, rumors about looters' actions ran rampant and impacted not solely on the response of repressive forces and other state agencies but also on the behaviors and feelings of New Orleans common folks (*Times Picayune, New York Times, Guardian*). The reader should bear these three dimensions in mind as we move into the heart of the 2001 lootings. What appears as chaotic violence, in both New Orleans and Argentina, is simply incomprehensible if we do not pay simultaneous attention to the diverse degrees of organization among perpetrators, to their relationships (not always oppositional) with repressive forces, and to the role played by rumors. Let me then briefly describe these three dimensions for the case of post-Katrina New Orleans. They anticipate some of the crucial elements in the unfolding of collective violence during the 2001 lootings in Argentina. A summary description is then in order so that the reader can recognize some familiar aspects as we move into the less-known terrain of the Argentine episodes.

Looting Together   Looting was not the action of isolated individuals but of groups. As the chief of homeland security for New Orleans, Col. Terry Ebert, put it on August 31 (*New York Times*, August 31, 2005): "We have a major looting problem. These are not individuals looting; these are groups of armed individuals." St. Bernard Parish Sheriff Jack Stephens echoed Ebert: "Small gangs of heavily career criminals are roaming the parish's isolated eastern half and looting buildings" (*Times Picayune*, September 5, 2005).[7] Exaggerations aside (weeks after the events, some of the reports about criminal gangs looting their way through entire neighborhoods proved to be false), Ebert and Stephens were encapsulating one of the recurrent findings in studies of superficially anarchic collective violence: Lootings' main actors are clusters of people, not solitary individuals. As is true of many other types of collective violence, looting is a collective enterprise.

[7] See also the *Times Picayune* report on September 2, 2005a, speaking of looting "bands."

Looting with the Police   These groups are aided in their actions by police absence, inaction, and/or complicity.[8] That police absence or inaction facilitated the looting seems to be quite apparent, admitted even by police officers themselves. A report from the *New York Times* (September 1, 2005) written as the events were unfolding, reads: "With police officers and National Guard troops giving priority to saving lives, looters brazenly ripped open gates and ransacked stores for food, clothing, televisions sets, computers, jewelry and guns, often in full view of helpless law-enforcement officials." The Chief of New Orleans Homeland Security put it quite candidly the day after the major outbreak of looting: "The New Orleans police are almost completely involved in saving lives and not in guarding the city" (*New York Times*, August 31, 2005). Other reports from local newspapers repeat this assessment: when looting was about basic necessities, police officers "had a more pressing problem than people walking off with food and liquor" (*Times Picayune*, September 1, 2005b).[9]

Police officers acknowledge their own powerlessness in the face of crowds in search of basic provisions: "One of the officers who went to the Wal-Mart said the police did not try to stop people from taking food and water. 'People sitting outside Wal-Mart with groceries waiting for a ride, I just let them sit there,' said Sgt. Dan Anderson of the Sixth District. 'If they had electronics, I just threw it back in there" (*New York Times*, September 29, 2005). Outside Wal-Mart, people were couching their actions in terms of pressing needs and permissive police (in)action: "We need clothes and food . . . the police are letting everybody go in and get what they need. . . . They're not letting you get TV's and stuff, but the people are overpowering them." A firefighter present on the scene concurred: "There's not enough police to stop them" (*New York Times*, August 31, 2005).

Some reports, however, depict not simply police absence or incapacity but officers' participation in the looting. According to the *New York*

---

[8] This is not to say that police were completely passive. Several reports describe the attempts of the National Guard and the local police to stop the lootings, sometimes with great risk to their lives. A police officer was shot in Algiers (New Orleans) during a confrontation with a looter (*New York Times*, September 29, 2005).

[9] In this particular case, the report refers to the break-in of a Sports Authority that had a stockpile of guns and ammunition.

Introduction

Times, New Orleans Sixth District witnessed "heavy looting, with much of the stealing confined to the lower-income neighborhoods. A particular target was a Wal-Mart store on Tchoupitoulas Street." At that particular site, looters appeared to have followed "police officers into the store after they broke it open" (*New York Times*, September 29, 2005). Reporters from the *Times Picayune*, in turn, assert that some police agents "joined in with looters and marauders.... Some officers joined in grabbing supplies from breached stores, carrying off socks, T-Shirts, food and other essentials" (*Times Picayune*, September 4, 2005). As days went by, some of these reports proved to be true: On Thursday September 29, the New Orleans police acting superintendent Warren J. Riley "announced the suspension or reassignment of five officers suspected of looting or standing by as looting occurred" (*New York Times*, September 30, 2005). Seven others were being investigated (see also *USA Today*, September 29, 2005).

Looting Rumors   Rumors about invading hordes of looters ran rampant hours after the hurricane struck, shaping both police performance and residents' behaviors.[10] As Westwego police chief, Dwayne Munch, described: "Faced with reports that 400 to 500 armed looters were advancing on the town of Westwego, two police officers quit on the spot. The looters never appeared." And then, in a statement that could be applied beyond New Orleans, he asserted: "Rumors could tear down an entire army" (*New York Times*, September 29, 2005).

Police absence was sometimes filled in by the private repression of fearful residents, epitomized in the sign "You Loot, I Shoot," described in a report from *The Guardian*. This story summarizes one of the effects of the rumors quite well:

> As if water worries weren't enough ... now the looting is becoming an extremely serious problem. In Uptown, one of the few areas that remained dry, a bearded man patrolled Oak Street near the boarded-up Maple Leaf Bar, a sawn-off shotgun slung over his shoulder. The owners of a hardware store sat in folding chairs, pistols at the ready. "They broke

[10] On the "twisted stories" about violence that rapidly circulated during the first week after Katrina, see "America's Ordeal," published in the *Guardian* on September 4, 2005.

into the Shell station across the street," he said. "I walked over with my 12-gauge and shot a couple into the air." A supply store sported spray-painted signs reading "You Loot, I Shoot" and "You Bein' Watched." (*Guardian*, September 1, 2005a)

Another report from the *Times Picayune* (September 8, 2005) clearly depicts the effects of rapidly circulating rumors on the actions and feelings of individuals already traumatized by the hurricane. The fear of invading hordes of looters described in this report will find resonance in many of the stories heard and told by residents in Buenos Aires:

> Just after dusk on Tuesday night, with the rumble of helicopters and air-planes still overhead, Gareth Stubbs took his spot in a rocking chair on the balcony of an Algiers Point house, a shotgun, bottle of bug spray and a can of Pringles at his feet. It was night No. 9 of his vigil, the balcony turned into a makeshift watch tower, with five borrowed shotguns, a pistol, a flare gun, an old AK-47 and loads of ammunition strategically placed next to the blankets and pillows where Stubbs, Vinnie Pervel and Gregg Harris have slept every night since Hurricane Katrina slammed into Southeast Louisiana. . . . It's been a terrifying nine days for the four, scrambling for food, water, and gasoline for their generator and an arsenal of weapons they feared they would need if complete lawlessness broke out in the his-toric neighborhood of renovated 19th century homes. The neighborhood having survived the storm without flood damage, Pervel and Harris, both former presidents of the Algiers Point Association, worried that looters and others seeking high ground would invade the community.

Only a month after the events, the *New York Times* (September 29, 2005) reported that "some, though not all, of the most alarming stories that coursed through the city appear to be little more than figments of fright-ened imaginations, the product of chaotic circumstances that included no reliable communications, and perhaps the residue of the longstanding raw relations between some police officers and members of the public." And yet, despite many of them being false, rumors gave form to police and residents' behaviors and sentiments in the immediate aftermath of Katrina.

In the influential circulation of rumors, in the groupness of looters, and in the facilitating role played by the police, post-hurricane loot-ings resemble many other such episodes around the world. Striking parallels will emerge as we dissect post-adjustment lootings in contemporary Argentina.

Collective Violence Scholarship

Food riots or lootings were once the preferred subject of collective behavior approaches (Cornelius 1969; Gurr 1970; Hibbs 1973; Lofland 1981; Turner and Killian 1987). In its emphasis on preexisiting ties and organizations, brokerage efforts, and elite certification, this book will join the warranted criticisms that have been launched against several of these collective behavior perspectives (McCarthy and Zald, 1971, 1977; Jenkins 1983; Tilly 1978; McAdam 1982).

Riots – both "race" and ethnic ones – have been widely researched in U.S. scholarship, mainly focusing on the 1968 wave following the assassination of Martin Luther King, Jr., and on the 1992 episodes in Los Angeles (see, for example, Stark et al. 1974 and Baldassare 1994; for different comprehensive reviews, see McPhail and Wohlstein 1983 and Useem 1998). There are plenty of now-classic studies on the individual attributes of participants in riots (Caplan 1970; Caplan and Paige 1968; Moinat et al. 1972), as well as classic and contemporary studies on the demographic, economic, ethnic, and racial composition of rioting communities (Spillerman 1970; Lieberson and Silverman 1965; Wohlenberg 1982; Bergensen and Herman 1998). One of the strengths of this U.S-based scholarship is its emphasis on the complexity, diversity, interactive, and dynamic character of lootings. This book applies these insights to a phenomenon heretofore unexamined. In particular, I will draw on two key insights of this body of literature: (a) *the relational underpinnings of lootings*: contrary to common (mis)understandings that speak of "anarchic" outbursts, riots are carried out in small groups of people who are connected in some ways (through friendship, family, and/or community ties) and assemble, remain, and disperse together (Aveni 1977; McPhail and Wohlstein 1983); (b) *the selectivity of looters' actions*: far from being random collective actions, looters selectively target particular kinds of stores (based on the ethnicity of the store owner, the type of store, and/or other variables) (Rosenfeld 1997; Tierney 1994).

With the notable exceptions of the seminal studies by Walton and Seddon (1994) and Walton and Shefner (1994), food riots in Latin America have not been examined with the same degree of theoretical sophistication and empirical rigor. Walton and Seddon (1994) analyze the wave of popular protest that followed the implementation of structural adjustment policies and government austerity measures in the developing world from the 1970s to the 1990s (for a more general statement, see Walton and Ragin 1990). These authors contend that the specific origin of "austerity protests" [i.e., "large-scale collective actions including political demonstrations, general strikes, and riots" (1994:39)] lies in the period of global adjustment that ensued after the international debt crisis. Walton and Shefner apply this same global approach to their analysis of the generalization of protest highlighting, at the same time, some important mediating factors. During the 1990s, a decade that witnessed a "global trend toward neo-liberal economic reorganization," they assert that "[t]he broad implementation of austerity measures as a condition of structural adjustment and debt restructuring represented an attack on the very means that made urban life sustainable. Austerity led to popular protest in the times and places that combined economic hardship, external adjustment demands, hyperurbanization, and *local traditions of political mobilization*" (1994:99, my emphasis). My analysis of the 2001 lootings will complement and specify this previous research by (a) examining the internal dynamics of riot episodes rather than their structural causes (a task actually hinted at when these authors gathered case-based evidence; see specifically Walton 1989); and (b) scrutinizing the political dimensions of rioting (an important complement to the more structural analysis).

Europeanist social historians have paid sustained attention to the *political makings* of food riots (i.e., to the impact that relationships between active participants in food lootings and established authorities have on the origins and course of the episodes). Note that I am not speaking about the riots' political *significance* – a hotly debated topic among historians of Europe (see, for example, Rudé 1964; Thompson 1994; see also Bouton 1993 for a review of the debate) and sociologists doing research on the 1968 and 1992 U.S. riots (see, for example, Gooding-Williams 1993) – but about the riots' political *genesis* (i.e., the bearing that ties between looters and authorities *before and during the episodes* have in their development).

In his study of riots in England and Wales at the turn of the eighteenth century, for example, Bohstedt (1983) asserts that we should look at the strength and stability of both horizontal networks (relations between members of a community that are based on kinship, market, neighborhood) and vertical networks (relationships between that community and the elites and authorities) in order to understand and explain the episodes. Riots, in Bohstedt's view, were expressions of community politics. Cynthia Bouton's (1993) examination of the French Flour War also highlights the political side of food riots. In a paragraph that will find great resonance as we move into the heart of the December 2001 episodes, she notes the ambiguous role played by local authorities and notables:

> Standing between hostile camps of consumers and merchants and producers, local authorities became pivotal figures in confrontations that revolved around subsistence crises. Although preserving order constituted a primary duty – a duty that included arresting and punishing those who disturbed the public order – village, municipal, and even royal authorities frequently sympathized with the plight of distraught consumers and sometimes actually collaborated with rioters, even when protests engendered violence. For example, we find them turning a blind eye to crowds that stopped merchants from moving supplies, assisting in the price-fixing and distribution of grain obtained by popular forces or threats, joining and sometimes leading rioting crowds, and protecting individuals accused of violent actions. (1993:5)

Bouton (1993), Thompson (1994), and Markoff (1996) also bring to light an aspect of the eighteenth-century European subsistence riots that will prove key to understanding and explaining the dynamics of the 2001 lootings in Argentina: the close and crucial relationship between the workings of patronage networks and the development and outcome of riots, between established ways of doing politics and extraordinary ways of expressing collective suffering.[11]

---

[11] Breakdown theories of collective action are, according to Bert Useem (1998), still useful to explain collective actions that involve a basic rupture of the social order (akin to the 2001 food riots). Given the continuities between ordinary politics and extraordinary violence that, as we will see, exist in the case of the December lootings, the strict

The political causes of collective violence are also highlighted in Steven Wilkinson's recent *Votes and Violence* – to my knowledge, the most systematic study of the connections between electoral competition and ethnic riots. Wilkinson convincingly shows that "ethnic riots, far from being relatively spontaneous eruptions of anger, are often *planned* by politicians for a clear electoral purpose. They are best thought of as a solution to the problem of how to change the salience of ethnic issues and identities among the electorate in order to build a winning political coalition" (2004:1, my emphasis). Throughout his detailed and insightful study, Wilkinson calls attention to the instances in which political elites "cause," "foment," or "instigate" riots "in order to win elections" (2004:236). His study brings to the fore the state's complicity in failing to prevent violence: "[T]he response of the state government is the main factor in determining whether large-scale ethnic violence breaks out and continues" (2004:62). This response, he argues, is very much conditioned by the "instructions" given by politicians to state officials telling them "whether to protect or not protect minorities" (2004:65, 85). According to Wilkinson, "the number of Hindu–Muslim riots seems to vary dramatically depending on the orders given by the political party in power" (2004:65). Political elites and organizers "incite" violence and prevent repressive forces from acting once riots break out. Why? Wilkinson's conclusions are straightforward: Some political leaders in some Indian states "impress upon their local officials that communal riots and anti-Muslim pogroms must be prevented at all costs" (2004:137) because they have the electoral incentives to do so. As he puts it, "States with higher degrees of party fractionalization, in which minorities are therefore pivotal swing voters, have lower levels of violence than states with lower levels of party competition. This is because minorities in highly competitive party systems can extract promises of greater security from politicians in return for their votes" (2004:137).

In its attention to the role of political organizers, state authorities, and repressive forces, my examination of the 2001 lootings dovetails

division between routine and nonroutine forms of collective action that breakdown theory emphasizes is unwarranted. Simply put, breakdown theories are not useful tools with which to understand, much less explain, what happened during the 2001 lootings in Argentina.

with Wilkinson's emphasis on the political causes of violence. My analysis, however, pays closer consideration to the actions and views of the actual perpetrators of violence before, during, and after the episodes in order to inspect (a) the micromechanisms and processes that generate massive destruction; (b) damage-makers' understandings of the political underpinnings of the violence; and (c) the ways in which participants make sense of (and justify) their own violent actions.

Existing scholarship insists on the rootedness of collective violence in "normal" social relations (Piven and Cloward 1979; Rule 1988), on the multifarious ways in which violent contention takes place embedded, and often hidden, in the mundane structures of everyday life and routine politics (Roy 1994; Brockett 2005). Tilly (1992:6) writes: "Contentious gatherings obviously bear a coherent relationship to the social organization and routine politics of their settings. But what relationship? That is the problem."[12] Drawing on recent developments in the scholarship on collective violence (Wilkinson 2004; Tilly 2003; Roldán 2002; Volkov 2002; Blok 2001; Brass 1996, 1997; Kakar 1996; Das 1990), this book addresses precisely this problem by focusing on party brokers and police agents (and their oftentimes obscure, clandestine relations) as key connectors between everyday politics and extraordinary collective action.

Once we focus empirical attention on the looting dynamics, and on the mechanisms and networks that played a role in their making, we begin to detect the existence of a gray zone where the analytical distinctions that the literature on collective action takes for granted (among government agents, repressive forces, challengers, polity members, etc.) collapse. I faced a difficult problem in reconstructing what actually happened during December 2001, when repressive forces did not "repress" but, sometimes, looted; when looters were aided in their damaging actions by state actors; and when the relationships between looters and authorities were seemingly so intense that it was hard to analyze them as different actors. This had to do with the fact that most of the categories that we, as scholars of collective action, routinely operate with (categories that are very

[12] Or, as Piven and Cloward (1979:20–1) write, "it is the daily experience of people that shapes their grievances, establishes the measure of their demands, and points out the targets of their anger."

much informed by empirical analyses carried out in the United States and Europe) proved useless, if not misleading. As much as the literature agrees that the *interactions* between political elites, agents of social control, and protagonists of civil disorder matter, these remain discrete entities (for a paradigmatic example, on U.S. riots, see Useem 1997; but see Goldstone 2003 for a recent exception). The imaginary political anthropology of social movement and collective action scholarship lives in a world in which there are clear boundaries between insurgents and authorities, dissidents or challengers and state actors, located in different regions of the social and political space: the "protest side" and the "repression side" (McPhail and McCarthy 2005:3; see Earl, Soule, and McCarthy 2003; Gamson 1990 [1975]). In point of fact, a recent illuminating collection devoted to studying the dynamic interactions between repression and mobilization (Davenport, Johnston, and Mueller 2005) remains silent about the possible participation of authorities (either elected officials or police agents) in the direct promotion of mobilization and/or the straightforward perpetration of collective violence. In part, the notion of the gray zone of clandestinity seeks to address this problem.

Boundaries between institutionalized and noninstitutionalized politics are "fuzzy and permeable" (Goldstone 2003:2). State institutions and political parties are often deeply penetrated by social movements, "often developing out of movements, in response to movements, or in close association with movements" (Goldstone 2003:2). In other words, "far from being separate domains, institutional politics and movement actions are deeply intertwined... their relationships are not reducible simply to action and response, opportunity and repression" (Goldstone 2003:24). Recent work around the dynamic interpenetration between state actions, the emergence and strategies of political parties, and social movements highlights the fact that groups and individuals who engage in protest (violent or not) may also, later in time, work for political parties, run for office, or occupy government posts to pursue their goals. The very same people can be "outsiders" – sometimes engaging in illegal or violent protest – and, soon after, "insiders" – actively participating in institutional politics. The notion of the gray zone highlights the fact that the lines between insurgents and state agents and party activists are *also* dissolving in the *opposite direction*. Party activists and state agents (police) may accept (and sometimes encourage and direct) collective violence. As we will see, insiders and outsiders appear in the realm of looting, blurring the lines between institutional and noninstitutionalized politics and making the latter seem simply a mode of the former.

In and Out: Looters in Their Places and Cubist Fieldwork

This project began as an attempt to understand and explain the dynamics of the 2001 lootings. The first step was to reconstruct in as complete detail as possible what happened between December 14 and December 22, 2001. In order to do so, I created a catalog of the events with information culled from several sources. I read four national newspapers (*Clarín*, *Crónica*, *La Nación*, and *Página12*) for the days of the lootings (both the printed and on-line editions), the month before and the year after the episodes. I also read ten local newspapers (from the provinces where lootings occurred – *El Ciudadano*, *La Voz del Interior*, *La Mañana del Sur*, *Rio Negro*, *Cronica-Chubut*, *La Gaceta*, *El Litoral*, *El Liberal*, *Los Andes*, and *El Sol*) covering the months of December 2001 and January 2002, and the October, November, and December 2001 and January 2002 issues of *Para Ud!*, a local newspaper printed in Moreno (Buenos Aires). For the purposes of data collection, I considered a looting episode to be the activity of two or more persons either (a) forcibly seizing objects in spite of restraint or resistance or (b) attempting to seize objects but meeting with effective restraint or resistance.

In the creation of this catalog I relied mainly on "hard news items" (i.e., the who, what, when, and where of the episodes), which, as other researchers have pointed out, are generally more precise than "soft news" (i.e., journalists' impressions and inferences) (see Earl, Soule, and McCarthy 2004:72). Throughout this book, it becomes clear that journalistic accounts of the events were far from accurate and reliable; a limitation that has been pointed out several times by social movement scholars and that is even more serious in the case of episodic violent collective action.[13] Despite its shortcomings, however, the catalog helped

---

[13] See, among others, Franzosi (1987), Myers (1997), Bessinger (1998), Koopmans and Rucht (1999, 2002), Earl et al. (2004), Myers and Schaefer Caniglia (2004).

me to create a statistical model of the relationships between looting sites, the number of participants in the lootings, the presence or absence of the police and party brokers (see Appendix). Occasionally, I will make reference to the model of interactions between looters, repressive forces, and party brokers that emerges from the newspaper accounts. In a nutshell, the model created with the newspaper data tells the following story: *The number of looters did not have an impact on police presence; police forces protected large markets as opposed to small ones; and brokers tended to be present at small market lootings when there were no police around.*[14] Despite its deficiencies (or probably because of them), the model served to discipline my qualitative inquiry, guiding the very specific research operations (in-depth interviews with witnesses, participants, and officials; analysis of investigative journalists' reports; even informal conversations with party brokers) that went into it.[15]

The analysis that follows is also based on three reports about the lootings that were published by investigative journalists (Bonasso 2002; Camarasa 2002; Young 2002) and on the video archives of *Canal 11*, a major national TV channel, where I was able to watch the reports and the images (some of them never broadcast) that were produced at the time of the events. But the bulk of the account that follows is based on fieldwork at two sites where some of the heaviest looting activity in Buenos Aires took place. Fieldwork comprised in-depth interviews and informal conversations with residents of the poor barrios Lomas Verde (in the district of Moreno) and BID (in the district of La Matanza). Both barrios are located roughly the same distance (13 and 15 blocks, respectively) from two commercial strips that were seriously damaged during the lootings: *El Cruce de Castelar* in Moreno and the crossroads

---

[14] For an account of the lootings based on statistical analysis of the catalog, see Auyero and Moran (2007).

[15] On the key role of formalisms in the research process, see Tilly (2004). Along the same lines, Doug McAdam (2003:285) calls for qualitative fieldwork in the study of collective action that reverses the usual order between quantitative and qualitative research. As he asserts, "Quantitative analysis can be used, as it has been in the study of social movements, to uncover consistent empirical relationships, that can be interrogated more fully using systematic qualitative methods." That is pretty much the order in which my own research proceeded, from statistical modeling of the relationships between looters, brokers, police, and looting sites, based on newspaper accounts, to qualitative research on looting dynamics.

Introduction

of Crovara and Cristianía Streets in La Matanza. I chose both neighborhoods after a month or so of preliminary research that indicated that people from both enclaves had participated in the lootings. With the help of two research assistants, I conducted sixty interviews with residents of both barrios. A third of these residents did loot, and two-thirds of them were able to provide detailed descriptions of what went on during the week under investigation, even if they had not taken part in the events. In both neighborhoods, we asked similar questions of the residents. We asked them about their job situation during the month of December 2001 (whether or not they had jobs and, if so, whether or not they went to work during that week) and about their ways of making ends meet during the month before the lootings (we paid particular attention to the kind of state assistance they were receiving and if there had been any interruptions in the delivery of welfare programs during the preceding months). We also inquired about their daily routines during the day the lootings started (How did they find out about the events? What did they do when they did find out?) and about their neighbors' actions during the episodes (making sure they felt safe about telling stories by assuring them that we did not want to know specific names of people). If they said they went to the looting sites, we asked them whether they went by themselves or with somebody else, about the goods they brought with them, and about the actions of the police (we asked them whether or not they were scared and whether or not it was their first time in a looting). We then focused attention on the targets: How did they decide which store was worth entering? Were the owners or managers there? How did they react? We also reported what other people had told us about the lootings (i.e., that they had been organized, preplanned) and asked them about their opinions concerning that statement (Were there organizers and/or brokers among the crowds?). Lastly, we asked them about the days that followed the lootings (What did they do? What did their neighbors say about the episodes?) and about their opinions of the victims of the violence (What did they think about the owners of the looted stores?). The last (and the only "why") question in every interview was the same: Why do you think the lootings happened?

We also interviewed twenty store owners, managers, and employees at each site. Half of them worked in stores that were looted, and half of them worked at stores that were spared from the violence. We asked the same questions of them: What did they remember about those days? Was your store looted or not? If their stores were sacked, we asked them to provide as detailed descriptions as possible of what they witnessed and how they felt at the time. In the case of the stores that were not sacked, we asked them to describe their actions and thoughts during that week (If they stayed inside the stores as many others did, what did they do? If they tried to pay for extra police protection, how did they contact the police agents? If they armed themselves, what specific actions did they take?). We then asked them (a) whether or not they knew the looters; (b) whether the looters were customers or not; (c) whether they saw the looters after the violence ended; and (d) whether or not there were organizers among the looters. We also asked them if they had received any sort of indemnification from the local, provincial, or federal state. Finally, we also asked the "why" question that we had formulated for looters: Why do you think the lootings happened?

The research started as a case study: an attempt to study looters as they moved from their neighborhoods to the looting scenes and as they moved from being poor residents to being looters – from *barrios* to *saqueos*, from *vecinos* to *saqueadores*. In other words, the inquiry started as a study of, to paraphrase from (and extend) Zussman's (2004) evaluation of qualitative work, *people in and through places*. And yet, the more I scrutinized the lootings at both sites, the more I became interested in a region of the social and political space that, expressed in full during the lootings, does not disappear once the violence subsides. This shift in interest is implied in the very logic of the case study. As Zussman (2004:362) writes, "Successful case studies look at extremes, unusual circumstances, and analytically clear examples, all of which are important not because they are representative but because they show a process or a problem in particularly clear relief."[16] In other words, initially the lootings were constructed as a case that would serve to extend theoretical work on the dynamics of collective violence (Burawoy 1998; Snow, Morrill and Anderson 2003;

---

[16] For the logic and relevance of case studies, see Ragin and Becker's (1992) classic; see also Alford (1998) and Katz (2001, 2002).

Introduction

Tilly 2003) by pointing at the role of (and interactions between) specific actors in its making. As I progressed in my fieldwork, I realized that the collective violence that visited people and places during December 2001 had accentuated and synthesized, as a sort of really existing ideal type, "a great many diffuse, discrete, more or less present and occasionally absent concrete individual phenomena" (Weber 1949:90) that existed (and still do) in the normal course of political life. Thus, my initial interest in "the case" was complemented by a focus on what I here call "the gray zone" – the area of clandestine relationships where routine politics converges with extraordinary violence. This led me to expand the research in time and space – including previous fieldwork experiences that contained interesting stories about this theme as well as current ethnographic work that, although on a different subject, retains a preoccupation with everyday politics. This book thus incorporates insights from my past and current fieldwork in two Argentine provinces (Neuquén and Santiago del Estero) and in two poor neighborhoods on the outskirts of Buenos Aires (Avellaneda and Lanús), together with interviews that I conducted specifically for this project with several informants (grassroots leaders, journalists, local officials, and politicos). The strategy was to pile up evidence regarding the looting dynamics and the existence and workings of the gray zone, triangulating as much as possible the available different sources of information with each other. The result would probably not stand up in a court of law, but, I hope, it will achieve a sound understanding and explanation of the complex political dynamics of collective violence.

Cubism would then probably be the best definition of the fieldwork that I ended up carrying out once the analytical interests expanded and of the kind of narrative that lies ahead.[17] Fieldwork and writing (combining analytical and narrative styles) helps to replicate the elusive character of the object under investigation. While the *empirical* object is the peak of collective violence during December 2001, the *analytic* object is an

---

[17] I first heard about Cubist fieldwork from Jack Katz at a conference in my home institution. In more than one way, his talk inspired me to pursue this project. Two of his books, *Seductions of Crime* and *How Emotions Work*, are prime examples of this type of sociological research and narrative.

area – so central during the lootings but also key in routine politics – where the deeds and networks of violent entrepreneurs, political actors, and law enforcement officials secretly meet and mesh. Through a series of vignettes culled from past and present ethnographic fieldwork and from secondary sources, the narrative moves *in and out* of the lootings to shed light on the junction between the ordinary and the extraordinary or, to quote from Jean and John Comaroff, on the "mingling between the prescribed and the contingent" (Comaroff and Comaroff 1992:38). This book thereby takes heed of Cubism's main lesson: The essence of an object is better (or probably only) captured by showing it simultaneously from multiple points of view. Rather than a single point of view (the author's) on a single empirical object (the lootings), the text presents different planes that, as in Cubism, interlock to constitute a painting – here, the depiction of the gray zone, a region of the social and political space that despite the lack of much sustained scholarly consideration remains a central component in contemporary Latin American politics.

The preceding methodological and narrative caveats are in order because parts of the empirical universe under analysis here are usually hidden from view. It took me a while to figure out the actual sequence of events through which, for example, a resident (from being at home, cooking a meal, or watching TV) became a looter. Even after triangulating and cross-checking the information (contrasting testimonies of participants, bystanders, victims, reporters, etc.), there are many issues around which uncertainty prevails (for example: What, exactly, was the relationship between some brokers and some members of the police force?). This is not to say that "reality" (the food riot, in this case) does not exist outside of the discourses that seek to represent it, but to emphasize that our (or at least, my) knowledge of that reality (especially the episodic form that constitutes the empirical heart of this book) is limited. What follows is not a postmodern portrait of languages of violence but a social scientific analysis of the place of clandestine connections in the making of collective violence and in the operation of routine politics. Good analysis hinges on hard-labored (and as good as I was possibly able to accomplish) reconstruction. The why of collective violence (and of the gray zone) is in the how.

Introduction

Roadmap

As said, Cubism refers not only to an analytic strategy but also to the form in which evidence is presented. This book combines two different forms of writing: analytic and narrative. A forewarning to the reader is then in order: In pursuit of "the-hard-to-pin-down" gray zone, the text that follows resembles a collage where I intercalate field notes and interview excerpts, close-up descriptions of particular processes, and reconstructions of noteworthy events and/or viewpoints of key actors.[18]

This first chapter summarizes the existing literature on what I term, following Primo Levi, the gray zone of politics and provides several examples of the form it takes *in practice* in contemporary Argentina. Party brokers are this region's key figures. In Chapter 2, I describe their actions and networks in detail. The third chapter situates the December 2001 lootings in the context of a region that has witnessed its share of rioting activity in the past decade. It then provides a straightforward empirical description of the geographic distribution of the 2001 lootings and their diversity. This description is mostly based on secondary resources (newspaper accounts, media images, and investigative journalists' reports). In this chapter, I analyze different types of looting scenes and call attention to the relationality of the violence, a relationality that takes center stage in the following chapter. The fourth chapter moves into the heart of two looting sites. Drawing on in-depth interviews with looters, the looted, bystanders, grassroots leaders, and public officials, it describes the unfolding of violence in Moreno and La Matanza and highlights the existence of three mechanisms that, usually present in other types of collective action (McAdam, Tarrow, and Tilly 2001; Tarrow 2005; Tilly 2003), were crucial during these episodes. These are (1) the creation of opportunities jointly carried out by party brokers and police agents, (2) the implicit validation of looting by state elites, and (3) the signaling spirals carried out by party brokers. Analytically, my account disaggregates the episodes in two (the production of opportunities to loot and the taking advantage of those opportunities) and focuses most of the attention on the former.

---

[18] Much of the inspiration for this style of writing came from Wacquant's excellent book, *Body and Soul*.

Lootings are usually characterized in the press and in many scholarly accounts as cases of "opportunistic" collective violence, episodes in which "as a consequence of shielding from routine surveillance and repression, individuals or clusters of individuals use immediately damaging means to pursue generally forbidden ends" (Tilly 2003:15). The description of different episodes and the dissection of two particular instances of looting will show us that these events are not simply cases of collective opportunism, but that they share key elements with other types of inter-personal violence. The closer we look at the lootings, the more we see "broken negotiations" in their midst [forms of collective action that pro-duce resistance "to which one or more parties respond by actions that damage persons and/or objects" (Tilly 2003:16)]. More surprising is the fact that a meticulous examination of their unfolding hints at elements of "coordinated destruction" [where persons and/or organizations "that specialize in the deployment of coercive means undertake a program of damage to persons and/or objects" (Tilly 2003:14)].

In the last chapter, I examine the lootings' aftermath by describing the emotions and moral reflections that were triggered by the episodes among looters and the looted. The overall aim here is to understand how participants make sense of collective violence. These interpretations pro-vide insightful commentaries on the workings of institutions and party politics in contemporary Argentina. In this chapter, we see victims and perpetrators talking about justice and injustice, about fairness and unfair-ness, about the failures and duties of authorities to help and/or protect them. The reader, in other words, is confronted with the voices of peo-ple talking, profusely, about political power. Years after the events, these voices certainly contain elements of retrospective analysis (the looted sometimes describe what happened at the time using evidence that only emerged after the episodes) and retroactive justification (looters ratio-nalize their, even to them sometimes incorrect, actions). What is striking, however, is that all of them, far from *avoiding politics* in their recounting of the events and their aftermath (Eliasoph 1998), talk almost exclusively about (party and state) politics. Different from other settings, victims and perpetrators discuss their everyday problems (before and after the lootings), the sources and possible solutions, not in the language of kin-ship (Lomnitz 1975), religion (Semán 2000), witchcraft (Ashforth 2005;

28

Stoller 2004), and/or economic ambition or personal merits (Bourgois 2003; Dohan 2003; Edin and Lein 1997; Ehrenreich 2002) but in the language of politics. In the last chapter, I reflect on the substance of this political talk as a window into people's moral universes.

This was not an easy book to write – not only because of the amount of fieldwork entailed and the sometimes-exhausting emotional toll caused by long and difficult conversations with perpetrators and victims of violence. It was a thorny task because I kept (and still keep) adjusting the vision as I was doing the research and, even more so, as I was writing (I think I finally understood how complex the process of "constructing a sociological object" is). The more I looked into the lootings, the more I saw gray dimensions of it. And the more I reflected on past and present fieldwork along gray lines, the more certain aspects of the lootings became more intriguing. If, by the end of this Cubist journey, the reader comes out with a better understanding of the lootings *and* with a greater sensibility toward an area of politics that is all-too-often neglected, this book will have accomplished its mission.

1

The Gray Zone

Primo Levi (1988:38) describes the shock experienced by the newly arrived at the Lager concentration camp in the following way:

> The world into which one was precipitated was terrible, yes, but also indecipherable: it did not conform to any model; the enemy was all around but also inside, the "we" lost its limits, the contenders were not two, one could not discern a single frontier but rather many confused, perhaps innumerable frontiers, which stretched between each of us. One entered hoping at least for the solidarity of one's companions in misfortune, but the hoped-for allies, except in special cases, were not there; there were instead a thousand sealed off monads, and between them a desperate covert and continuous struggle.

The world into which one was thrown was far from simple, he says, because it could "not be reduced to the two blocs of victims and persecutors" due to the existence of a "hybrid class of the prisoner-functionary" (Primo Levi 1988:37). The privilege enjoyed by certain prisoners and the collaboration they provided to the camp authorities constitute the Lager's "armature and at the same time its most disquieting feature. It is a gray zone," Levi writes, "poorly defined, where the two camps of masters and servants both diverge and converge. This gray zone possesses an incredibly complicated internal structure and contains within itself enough to confuse our need to judge" (Primo Levi 1988:42). This gray zone, Levi asserts, is a zone of ambiguity that challenges the pervasive we-they/friend-enemy bipartition; a Manichean tendency, "which shuns half-tints and complexities: it is prone to reduce the river of human occurrences to conflicts, and the conflicts to duels – we and they"

(Primo Levi 1988:37). The gray zone is, in Levi's mind, not simply an actual region in the social space of the concentration camp. It is also, and most importantly for the purposes of this book, a conceptual tool that warns us against too rigid – and misleading – dichotomies; in our case, looters, on one side, authorities and the looted on the other.[1]

Much like in the real life of the concentrations camps described in painstaking detail by Primo Levi, things before, during, and after the looting are messier than they actually look. There is, indeed, a gray area where the activities of those perpetrating the violence and those who presumably seek to control them coalesce. Scrutinizing this gray area not only allows us to better understand the dynamics of these particular lootings, it also, and here's the overall aim of this book, serves *to integrate "extraordinary" collective violence into the study of "normal" politics.* Much like Levi, then, I conceive of the gray zone as both an empirical object and an analytical lens that draws our attention toward a murky area where normative boundaries dissolve, where state actors and political elites promote and/or actively tolerate and/or participate in damage-making.

Although far from being a clearly delimited area of inquiry, the gray zone of politics has attracted some, still scattered, scholarly attention. Research on the origins and forms of communal violence in Southeast Asia, for example, highlights the usually hidden links between partisan politics and violence. Writing about the new migrants who live on the margins of modern cities and their role in communal riots in the region, Veena Das asserts that the

> [I]nhabitants of these slums and "unauthorized colonies"...become a human resource for conducting the *underlife of political parties.* These are the people employed as strike-breakers; they make up crowds to

---

[1] In his breathtaking study of social suffering among homeless heroin addicts in San Francisco, California, Philippe Bourgois (forthcoming) uses the notion of the "gray zone" to capture the abusive behavior, personal betrayals, and self-inflicted damage that predominate in that specific universe. As becomes clear, in this book, I use the notion in a rather different way. The reference to life in concentration camps is not meant to introduce an analogy between state-sponsored totalitarian genocide and the kind of collective violence under study here. I make reference to Primo Levi's work because that is where I first encountered the notion of gray zone and because it highlights ambiguity and the lack of clear-cut boundaries between different areas of the social space.

demonstrate to the world the "popularity" of a particular leader; and they form instruments for the management of political opponents. It is not surprising then that in the organization of riots they should play a pivotal role in the perpetration of violence. (1990:12, my emphasis)

Along these lines, Shaheed's (1990) analysis of the Pathan-Mujahir conflicts during 1985–6 shows that the riots can be "traced directly to the actions of religious political parties." More recently Larissa MacFarquhar (2003) charts the existing connections between the head of the Hindu-nationalist Shiv Sena Party, Bal Thackeray, and anti-Muslim riots in contemporary India (see also Wilkinson 2004). Paul Brass's notion of "institutionalized riot systems" captures well these usually obscure connections: In these riot systems, Brass points out, "known actors specialize in the conversion of incidents between members of different communities into ethnic riots. The activities of these specialists [who operate under the loose control of party leaders] are usually required for a riot to spread from the initial incident of provocation" (1996:12). Sudhir Kakar's (1996) description of a *pehlwan* (wrestler/enforcer who works for a political boss) further illustrates the point: The genesis of many episodes of collective violence should be located in the area where the actions of political entrepreneurs and those of specialists in violence (people who control the means of inflicting damage on persons and objects) meet and mesh.

Jane and Peter Schneider's recent study of the Palermitan Mafia (2003) also calls for analytical attention to the ceaseless intertwining between state and party politics and organized collective violence.[2] Mafiosi shared with some state and political elites a moral and political space that Palermitans called the *intreccio*. As the Schneiders put it,

---

[2] In reconstructing the history of the Mafia, the authors examine its predecessors, bandits, and acknowledge that they "enjoyed the support of kin and neighbors, landed elites and notables, and the police" (Schneider and Schneider 2003:30). A similar statement can be found in one of the most attentive observers of Mafiosi, anthropologist and historian Anton Blok (2001:18): "Given the specific conditions of outlawry, bandits have to rely very strongly on other people. It is important to appreciate that all outlaws and robbers require protection in order to operate as bandits and to survive at all." For an insightful review of the debates sparked by Hobsbawm's work on social banditry among Latin Americanist scholars, see Joseph (1990). For further evidence on the intersection of politics and organized violence in Latin America, see Betancourt and García (1994).

[p]owerful elites – aristocratic and *civili* landowners occupying important political positions – protected mafiosi . . . shielding them from prosecution by the state. This relationship could take two forms – *favoreggiamento* and *manutengolismo*. The former refers to "favoring" . . . mafiosi with patronage, alibis, places to hide, and so on; the latter to directing or "using" them to accomplish one's own ends. (2003:31)

As the Schneiders understand it, the *intreccio* "signifies more than a simple reciprocity between mafiosi and the state; it points to a vast gray area where it is impossible to determine where one leaves off and the other begins" (2003:34).

Linda Krischke's (2000) work on transitions to multiparty politics in sub-Saharan Africa offers additional examples of the constant interweaving between party and state in the making of violence. Drawing on the cases of Cameroon, Kenya, and Rwanda in the 1990s, Krischke shows that ruling elites, when threatened by local opposition and forced into reform by external actors (these actors being other powerful states or lending agencies), resort to "informal repression" – that is, "covert violations sponsored by government authorities but carried out by third parties." They do so, she argues, in order to frustrate democratic transitions. As she writes, "a high level of conflict between regimes and their opponents, coupled with strong pressure to undertake a nominal democratic transition regardless of these relations, makes governments more likely to introduce informal repression" (Krischke 2000:384). The new means of coercion that endangered regimes are carried out by "surrogate bodies such as hit squads, party youth wings, and traditional leaders, against perceived and real government critics" (Krischke 2003:397). In other words, violent entrepreneurs [usually tied to patronage networks (Krischke 2003:398)] are in charge of the struggle to block the transitions to democracy. Among them, Krischke cites:

In Cameroon, *lamibe*, powerful government-appointed traditional chiefs in the primarily Muslim North, have provided an effective means of cover repression in that region. . . . In Rwanda, under President Habyarimana, the MRNDD and its extremist off-shoot, the Coalition pour la Défense de la République (CDR), both developed militias from their party youth wings, the *Interahamwe* and the *Impuzamugambi* respectively. Parallel to the militias, which drew on urban youth, a more elite death squad organization, "Network Zero," was run by high level security officers and members of the presidential entourage. In Kenya, "warriors" of Kalenjin and Maasai ethnicity, groups strongly represented in the ruling party, and more recently KANU "youthwingers" provided another mechanism of control by the state. (2003:398)

That party leaders and/or state officials (bureaucrats and/or police agents) might be "behind" – rather than against – episodes of collective violence should hardly surprise students of Latin American politics. In a detailed study of "la violencia" – as the wave of political violence that killed 200,000 people in Colombia in the 1940s and 1950s came to be known – historian Mary Roldán (2002:22) shows that in Antioquía "partisan conflict provided the initial catalyst to violence." She asserts that not only did state bureaucrats "promote" the violence that shocked the region but also that policemen and mayors actively participated in partisan attacks. She writes:

[V]iolence in peripheral areas (of Antioquía) was largely the product of concerted and systematic harrassment waged by selected regional authorities rather than the "natural" outgrowth of partisan conflicts among local residents . . . the regional state and its forces were the primary instigators of violence on the periphery. . . . Governors and their administrative subordinates played an extraordinarily important role in the promotion of partisan violence in Antioquía between 1946 and 1949. (Roldán 2002:22)

Political elites, she points out, did not simply tolerate or instigate the violence; they were its perpetrators. While party members organized attacks on places and peoples, police acted as partisan shock troops [for further evidence on the Colombian case, see also Braun's (1985) study of the violence during the 1948 Bogotazo that followed the assassination of liberal leader Gaitán]. In a statement that would ring familiar to those studying political violence in other parts of the world, Roldán (2002:82) points out that "while many citizens attributed the escalation of violence to the absence of official forces, these forces were so often the perpetrators of violence between 1946 and 1949 that one wonders why anyone bothered to suggest that the presence of the authorities could have been of much help."[3]

In the contemporary Americas, we have several ethnographic accounts of the gray zone of politics. Gunst's taxing exploration of Jamaican gangs shows the links that *posses* had with political parties during the 1980s and the usually violent outcomes of what she calls "mafia-style links" (1995:83). The origins of Jamaican drug gangs in New York can be found, Gunst argues, in the *posses*, which were, in fact, political group-ings armed by party leaders linked to Seaga or Manley. Goldstein's (2003) recent ethnography of *Felicidade Eterna*, a *favela* in Rio de Janeiro, pro-vides further evidence of the collusion between state actors (in her case, the police) and violent entrepreneurs (gang members associated with drug trafficking). In point of fact, one of the actors in the *favela*'s every-day life, the "police-bandit," points to the heart of the intimate rela-tions that exist between local cops and local gangs of small-scale drug traffickers – so "intimate" that the limits become confused and confus-ing.[4] When describing residents' opinions about the possible perpetrator of the recent murder of the brother of a *dono* (boss), Goldstein (2003: 188–90) writes:

> When asked, nobody was sure whether the executioners were bandits, police, or "police-bandits." The term "police-bandits," as used by the res-idents of Felicidade Eterna, referred to their own sense of the inescapa-bility of violence in their world. They were aware of the violence of the gangs and the normalized and routine corruption of the police, but police-bandit seemed to mean something more. It seemed to refer to the possibility that both of these entities inevitably played by the rules of revenge and personal reputation, and their blurring signaled the recog-nition by residents of the dysfunctionality of the justice system. . . . In the

---

[3] A similar point regarding the participation of party and state officials in the perpe-tration of violence was made a long time ago by Steffen Schmidt. In his study of the clientelist bases of political violence in Colombia, he wrote (1974:109): "Colombia's political violence . . . is in great part due to the existence of widespread, competitive, aggressive, patron-client based politics." On the connections between patronage net-works and interpersonal violence, see Villarreal (2002). The author makes a strong argument about the relationships between increased electoral competition, weakening patronage networks, and the (subsequent) increase in violent crime (homicide) during the transition to democracy in Mexico.

[4] For a vivid account of this as seen from the point of view of a *favelada*, see Gay (2005).

local vernacular, the term "police-bandit" captures the sense of the break-down of the rule of law in the poorest neighborhoods, making clear the corrupt nature of the police.

Finally, the ethnographic work recently carried out by Arias (2003, 2004) in three of Rio's *favelas* draws attention to the overlap between collective violence (in his case, associated with drug trafficking) and party politics (in his case, a modern version of patronage). In a summary version of *favelas'* history, Arias (2004:2) points out that "[i]n the 1980s, drug traf-fickers began to employ many *favela* residents in their operations, provid-ing needed assistance to the poor and fortifying their political leadership. Politicians, seeing the AMs' (*associacoes de moradores*, residents' associa-tions) growing fragility, worked more directly with traffickers to secure votes. During this period, AMs began acting as intermediaries between traffickers, residents, and state officials." The ongoing violence in Rio's *favelas*, famously portrayed in Fernando Meirelles' film *City of God*, is the outcome of the consolidation of the political power of drug gangs. This process, in turn, would not be possible to understand without examin-ing, as Arias does, the connections between different levels of the state, drug traffickers, and the *favelas'* residents. In his detailed and varied descriptions of violence in the *favelas* and of the individual and collec-tive efforts to confront it, one message emerges time and again: "Many bureaucrats, police, and politicians take kickbacks or otherwise work with traffickers to accomplish personal objectives [...] Corrupt state officials work with locally empowered delinquents to enrich themselves and win votes" (Arias 2004:3–4). The overlaps and interweavings between the actions of traffickers, members of neighborhood associations, and state officials prevent us from talking about "parallel politics" [as Leeds (1996) did when examining the constraints that drug lords posed to democratic authorities and community leaders at the local level during the late 1980s and early 1990s] and lead us to explore the illegal networks that link dif-ferent actors and create an area where it is difficult, if not impossible, as the Schneiders put it, to establish clear-cut boundaries.

So, what do all these examples have in common? They all portray the activation of clandestine connections between political actors. These clandestine connections are, all of them agree, crucial to understand both routine political life and extraordinary collective violence. As we will now see, these underhand, concealed interactions are also critical in Argentine politics.

The Argentine Gray Zone

There are plenty of reports on acts of intimidation to and physical attacks on political opponents in Buenos Aires and elsewhere carried out by beneficiaries of welfare programs and/or party members and/or loyalists to a party leader who are deployed as shock troops (Verbitsky 2002; Vales 2003a). Reports about suspected links between politicos, elected officials, and illegal networks (Lopez Echagüe 1996; Otero 1997) and about dangerous liaisons between police agents and criminal gangs – sometimes at the heart of episodes of collective violence such as prison riots (Kollmann, February 13, 2005, April 13, 2005) – also abound. Journalist Lucas Guagnini (October 19, 2003) provided a detailed account of the links between soccer gangs (the infamous *barrabravas*) and local authorities and politicos (mainly, but not exclusively, in greater Buenos Aires). *Barrabravas* work during the electoral campaigns painting walls with the names of the candidates, providing protection for candidates, and intimidating opponents: "They are the workforce that many a politician uses as shock troops and that they pay with tax money" [further evidence of the collusion between politics, crime, and police action can be see in Klipphan (2004)].

Together, all these accounts point to an *intreccio* between violent entrepreneurs, state actors, and political elites that is more than an ephemeral phenomenon. It seems to be built into the way in which routine politics operates in the country. But the political science and sociological literature on Argentina hardly notes it, as if it belongs to the terrain of mere anecdotes with no effect whatsoever on the workings of the institutions about which academics do care (i.e., political parties, parliaments, and state agencies). But effects it has. Take, for example, the case of the police of the province of Buenos Aires – a key actor in the making of the lootings and in the ways in which everyday politics are conducted in that crucial Argentine state. It is generally agreed that the police of the province of Buenos Aires have been involved in gambling, prostitution, drug dealing, kidnappings, and car theft for the past two decades (Rother, November 16, 2003; Isla and Miguez 2003; Binder 2004; Klipphan 2004). A former undersecretary of security in the state of Buenos Aires and a highly perceptive analyst of the state police's (mis)behavior asserts that there is a "perverse relationship between politics, crime and police action" (Sain 2004:87).

During the early 1990s, Sain (2002:85) asserts, the government of Buenos Aires made an explicit agreement with the state police: In order to attain "respectable levels of public safety," the government provided the police with a great amount of material and financial resources and an important degree of freedom of action (i.e., unaccountability). The state government also assured the police that it would not intervene on the illegal self-financing activities that had long been developed by the police. This "circuit of illegal self-financing," as Sain calls it (2002:86), is the product of the participation of key members of the police hierarchy in an "extended network of criminal activities that revolved around illegal gambling, prostitution, drug and arms trafficking, and robberies" (Sain 2002:86). In 1998, the Minister of Justice and Security of Buenos Aires, León Arslanián, admitted that reform attempts had been unsuccessful in dismantling the "clandestine collection (*recaudación clandestina*) that feeds the police system with resources that come from criminal activities" (Sain 2002:115).

Illegal and clandestine practices are thus institutionalized in the police force (Isla and Miguez 2003).[5] In her perceptive and detailed ethnographic account of shantytown life in Quilmes (Buenos Aires), anthropologist Nathalie Puex looks at this very same phenomenon as seen from the bottom-up, examining shanty-dwellers' perceptions of the connection between criminal and police activity as well as the actual linkages between shanty youngsters and authorities:

---

[5] The film *El Bonaerense* provides a very insightful and, according to the literature, accurate rendition of the way in which illegality is institutionalized in the police force. Learning to be a cop, the film shows, implies by necessity learning to be a delinquent – above and beyond the good intentions of new recruits.

For many shantytown residents (*villeros*) the cop is another thief (*chorro*), much like a politician. The police officer does not represent the law because he himself takes part in criminal activity. [This participation creates an] image of the police as both a repressive force and a provider of jobs. Most of the young delinquents in the shantytown "work" for the police; in other words, they are part of an illicit organization directed by policemen who offer work to these shanty youngsters. Many of these youngsters obtain their income through participating in this organization. (2003:66)

Together with the existing connections between crime and law-enforcement worlds, analysts also point out that there is an area in which both worlds intersect and interact with party politics. Part of the funds the Buenos Aires police collect from their illegal activities goes to finance itself; another part, observers affirm, helps to sustain the machine of the largest political party in the country, the Peronist Party. As Sain (2004:22) remarks: "the world of politics, the security system – mainly the police – and crime constitute three intimately linked instances." Or, as a former justice minister told the *New York Times*: "There are politicians who are thieves and finance their campaigns with money from police corruption" (Rother, November 16, 2003). It is no wonder that state initiatives to reform the Buenos Aires police (which took place during the mid- to late-1990s) met with the stubborn resistance of "Peronist local politicians, mayors and brokers (*punteros*), as well as those belonging to the Radical party" (Sain 2002:90). These groups "had a well-oiled relationship with the police machine" whose illegally obtained resources went, in part, to finance party activities (Sain 2002:90). Police forces are hardly the only ones participating in illegal actions; "important sectors of political parties, state bureaucracies, including the judicial branch, are involved in extended systems of corruption" (Isla and Miguez 2003:318). Noting the extent to which security forces are involved in crime, Isla and Miguez (2003:323) assert that police forces "function as a mafia organization (especially in Buenos Aires) that itself produces criminal violence."

Let us now look at two concrete examples of the intersection between everyday life, routine politics, and violence by drawing on examples from my own fieldwork in the provinces of Neuquén and Buenos Aires.

The Gray Zone

Travelogue: El Chofa and Daniel in the Gray Zone

"If you want to understand politics in Cutral-co you should talk with
El Chofa...do you know who he is? He is quite a character...you
should talk with him." Those were the words of a former mayor of
the municipality of Cutral-co, an oil town in the Argentine Patagonia,
where I conducted fieldwork during 2000 and 2001. At the time, I did
not know who El Chofa was nor his relevance to my study. A few weeks
later, after several of my interviewees in Cutral-co and neighboring Plaza
Huincul mentioned him, I quickly learned about his actions during the
protest episodes I was investigating (Auyero 2003). At the time, I read
all the newspaper reports related to his story; I also interviewed him and
the local attorney general who was in charge of the investigation of his
"case." What follows is a reconstruction – based on those newspaper
accounts and several interviews – of a moment in Justo Angel (a.k.a. "El
Chofa") Guzmán's life, a moment in which he stood in a spotlight and
underwent an intense media attention and scrutiny that illuminates the
existence and workings of the gray zone.

On August 14, 1996, the police besieged El Chofa's ranch in Plaza
Huincul after they got word that "Piturro" Aranda – a convicted mur-
derer who had escaped from the local prison – was hiding there.
On Chofa's ranch, the police found machine guns and other assorted
weapons, together with half a kilogram of cocaine. According to the
police, Piturro was a member of a gang – a *superbanda* headed by El
Chofa – that presumably smuggled drugs and weapons from Bolivia to
the Patagonic provinces. In the summer of 2001, the attorney general
who was the leading investigator in this case told me that Chofa's gang
also commanded a prostitution ring: "He was the Czar of drugs and
prostitution, he controlled the worst criminal activity in the area...he
was the number one criminal [*El era el criminal número uno de la zona*]."

The police got neither Chofa nor Piturro. They escaped minutes
before the police arrived – apparently tipped off by members of the
same force that was after them. A few days later, in an article entitled,
"Nobody wanted to capture 'El Chofa'," the local newspaper *La Mañana
del Sur* reported that "El Chofa – a fugitive who was by then gradually

becoming a novelistic character – may have been able to escape because some of those in charge of arresting him dragged their feet" (*LMS*, August 20, 1996:16). Citing judicial sources, the newspaper reported that police agents "had more than one link with or knowledge about El Chofa." The attorney general confirmed this version: "Guzmán had contacts with low-level police agents."

But Chofa's contacts did not stop at the lower echelons of the local police department. Together with the weapons and the drugs, the cops found a cell phone that belonged to the local municipality where, the public soon learned, El Chofa had been an employee for the past five years. This "top criminal" had been, in the recent past, "the chauffeur, the bodyguard and even the confidant" of many a local politician and/or authority (*LMS*, August 20, 1996:16). Local officials and politicians relied on him as an enforcer to do their "dirty work" – from distributing drugs among youngsters in exchange for their attendance at rallies to intimidating opponents.

"Chofa was very linked to men in power," a former mayor of Cutral-co told me. "He was the chauffeur of Carlos Rosso [who later became ministry of interior of the province], and he had a metallurgic shop that did jobs for the municipality. The kids that worked for him, some of them public employees, were petty criminals who, during electoral campaigns, formed groups to paint walls and put up posters for the candidates." This former mayor is now retired from politics. With not much at stake, he once told me (almost as a confession) the story of how he and El Chofa met. The following brief statement and his frank reply to my question reveal in luminous form the intricacies of the gray zone and the pernicious ways in which, even among well-intended people, it perpetuates itself:

> MAYOR: One of my closest collaborators was a good friend of Chofa, and he brought him to some of our meetings during the electoral campaign. I met him in one of those meetings, and since the very beginning we got along quite well. He might have been an outcast [*a marginal*], but he was a good person. One day, close to the elections, we were alone at my place – he used to stop by to drink *mate* – and he told me: "I will protect you, because you are going to win the elections, and these sons of bitches (referring to the mayor's opponents and Chofa's former employers) will

make your life hell. They really want to screw up you and your family. You have no idea of what they are capable of doing to you. But if they know I'm with you, they won't bother you. I'm going to ask you only one thing: when you become the new mayor, don't let me out [*no me dejés afuera*]. If they see my car parked in front of your house, they won't bother you, stay calm [*quedate tranquilo*]." We won, and we gave him work (the municipality contracted with his shop) [. . .]

JAVIER: Did you know who he was, what he was involved with, before you got in touch with him?

MAYOR: Yes, of course, but *I'd rather have had him as a friend.* (my emphasis)

While Chofa was still a fugitive, the rumors linking him with prominent local politicians were confirmed by his father who was interviewed by reporters from *La Mañana del Sur* (August 23, 1996:12–13). Don Justo Guzmán began saying that now that Chofa was not around to take care of things, he and his grandson would have take charge of Chofa's ranch in the countryside: "Many animals are dead, but we can't find the receipts to be reimbursed for the works he did for Copelco (the local public services company) and for the municipality of Cutral-co, and to obtain the wages that the municipality of Plaza Huincul owes him." That was the first time during the course of the interview that his father hinted at Chofa's political connections. Later, Don Justo became more explicit: "All his problems began when he got into politics, especially when he became a bodyguard. Chofa started when he was 16 or 17. All he did afterwards was because of that environment (*Todo lo que hizo después fue por estar en ese ambiente*)." And in quite unambigous terms, he added: "Politicians always used him, now they will have to fix this mess." The attorney general agreed with Chofa's father and with the former mayor when he told me that "El Chofa was raised by members of the political elites, he always hung around the most powerful members of the Movimiento Popular Neuquino [MPN, the governing party in the province]." "Chofa's history," his father concluded, "began with the MPN . . . until recently he would go to barbecues with local politicians . . . *estaba en la joda con los políticos.* [. . .] He has been so involved in politics that someone [referring to a politician] should solve this problem."

Politicians did not "solve the problem" – in part, because the mayor with whom he was working was impeached and his (and Chofa's) opponents took charge (rumors had it that his former boss now wanted Chofa in jail, punished for having deserted his faction). On March 9, 1997, after an eight-month-long chase, Justo "El Chofa" Guzmán – who not for nothing was known as "The Zorro" – was arrested by the local police after a cinematographic chase through the Patagonian fields. Chofa tried to escape on his motorcycle but apparently fell and badly injured his head. When the police found him, he had a gun and a rifle, and – according to the attorney general – "he told the cop who got him: 'Please, brother, kill me.'" He wasn't killed, and, despite the "sort of commotion" that his arrest produced "in the local political environment" and the rumors that said that "now a big fish will go down too" (*LMS*, March 10, 1997:16–17), no local politician or official was ever indicted in connection with El Chofa. One last piece of information encapsulates Chofa's ambiguous place: The minister of government, Carlos Rosso, in charge of the local police who captured him, had been Chofa's first boss.

For many residents with whom I spoke in 2000 and 2001 in Cutral-co and Plaza Huincul, El Chofa was a sort of Robin Hood ("When there was hunger, he would kill one of his cows and distribute beef for free"), a *bandido* who helped the poor but that, at the same time [and as many a *bandido* before him (Joseph 1990; Blok 2001)], enjoyed well-oiled connections with the powerful. Many people, including former officials, doubted that he had ever been the drug lord depicted by the media – the former mayor still thinks that, in fact, it was all a conspiracy to penalize Chofa for the betrayal of his former boss. When I interviewed him at his shop in March 2001 (where he and his employees were still manufacturing the metal lamp posts contracted by the local municipal government), he was just coming out of jail on probation and was logically reluctant to talk. (El Chofa finished primary school while in jail, and one of his teachers was kind enough to put me in touch with him. I suspect that the only reason he granted me an interview was to please her.) He denied any involvement in the drug business but he did confirm – without many words and without naming names – his participation in local politics as someone who "took care of things when told so." A detailed description of the "things" he took care of was out of the interview's bounds, but when I described what others had told me about his actions (his role as politicians' enforcer, his logistical support, with wine and marihuana, of groups of youngsters during a massive protest that had the elite's initial support), he smiled and said, "That's possible, that sounds plausible."[6]

Chofa's story might surprise and annoy some political scientists (most, however, would dismiss it as "anecdotal"), but it would hardly be news to Daniel. He lives with his sister, Jimena, in Flammable shantytown (real name, despite the irony) – a poor enclave located in Dock Sud, Buenos Aires, adjacent to a large petrochemical compound that houses Shell-Dapsa and Petrobras among other large companies. What follows is the transcript of part of a dialogue that the three of us had in July 2004. We were talking about their ways of making ends meet [i.e., their survival strategies in the face of persistent unemployment (neither of them have had a stable job in the past two years)]. Jimena began describing the use that Peronist brokers made of unemployment subsidies (see Chapter 2), and soon Daniel took over to depict, in detail, how politics work in the area.

> JIMENA: It's really difficult, because Daniel doesn't have a job or a *plan* [an unemployment subsidy known as *Plan Jefas y Jefes de Hogar* – Program Head of Households]. He can't even get a plan, because the punteros [brokers] here are all sons of bitches. They give you a subsidy and they keep 50 pesos (subsidies consist of $150 per month).
>
> JAVIER: Do they take money from you?
>
> JIMENA: Yes, they take the money…
>
> DANIEL: If you don't want to work, you get $100, and you have to give them $50.
>
> JIMENA: And if you go to work, you have to give them $20 or $30… the subsidy should be free, but do you know how many times they left me out? […] If the brokers asked me for $50 I would go and denounce them…
>
> DANIEL: No, no! Wait! Do you know how many brokers I know? Go and try to denounce them…

---

[6] As of 2004, Chofa's shop was still serving the local municipality (the current mayor now belongs to the Radical Party).

JAVIER: They cut you off the plan...

DANIEL: They cut you off...

[...]

JIMENA: You have to do what they say...

JAVIER: And who are the most important brokers around here?

DANIEL: There's a bunch of them. I can't give you their names... everybody knows who they are, even those at the top know who the *punteros* are. I was with [meaning, he worked for] Laborde (the former mayor). When there was a rally, they would come and look for me... [they would say] "Dani, there's money, there's a joint [marihuana], there's *merca* [cocaine]... get a group together." They came and looked for me, I swear: "There's money, pot, coke, get the gang. I'll bring the bus. There's *escabio* [alcohol]." I talked with Laborde like this, face to face, and he told me, "Bring this amount of people and I'll give you this and that..."

JIMENA: I think Laborde did more than the mayor we have now...

DANIEL: Yes, yes...

JAVIER: But he would also provide pot and *merca*...

JIMENA: Well, yes... in every place there's that. Tell me about a politician who doesn't have *merca*...

DANIEL: All of them! Here, when there's a rally, we get tired of attending. I play the instruments in the group, in *la comparsa* [the music band that plays at the rallies]... and they come and look for me.

JAVIER: Which party?

DANIEL: Any party...

JIMENA: The one that comes for you...

DANIEL: Any party... today for Cacho [the current Mayor], tomorrow for Laborde [the former Mayor].

[...]

DANIEL: With Laborde we *re-luqueabamos* (we had a lot of profitable work)...

JAVIER: What did you do?

DANIEL: Anything and everything...we placed ads, we painted walls [with the name of the candidates/party]. We picked up the truck, they gave us the money to buy the paint...Sometimes we got into gun fights with others...

JAVIER: How come you did that? For [owning] a wall?

DANIEL: Well...you know...it's all politics. You know, when you are painting, [you say] "This wall is mine," and then another group comes and paints on top. That's when the trouble begins (*Y ahí se arma quilombo*).

Though in different capacities and diverse degrees of involvement, El Chofa and Daniel are both located in the midst of the gray zone. Neither of the episodes referred to here involve members of the Peronist Party. El Chofa worked for members of the MPN, a local center-right populist party, and Daniel's story refers to his association with a progressive mayor who belonged to a left-of-center party that is now almost extinct. The Peronists do not have the monopoly over the gray zone – by any means. How typical are these stories? How locally representative are they? Anybody who takes the trouble to look at party activity in Argentina closely enough will soon realize that both stories are all too common: Routine politics (whether right or left, Peronist or not) overlap with violence, not only during electoral times but also – as Chofa's story attests – in the regular operation of party politics.

The conversation I had with Daniel and Jimena also exemplifies a second area of overlap, this time between routine party politics and everyday life. Their account of (and complaint about) the workings of one of the few welfare programs they can have access to is all too commonplace among the urban poor in Buenos Aires. According to CELS (2003) numerous beneficiaries of the *Plan Jefas y Jefes* have complained about the "charge" that they have to pay to have access to the program. According to Marín (2003:21), "clientelist networks keep representing determinant channels to assure access and permanence in the program." Admission and tenure in the plan remains, for many, a matter of political favor. In the following chapter, I delve more deeply into the intersection between party politics and everyday life by taking a closer look at the workings of the Peronist machine in tandem with the provision of welfare programs

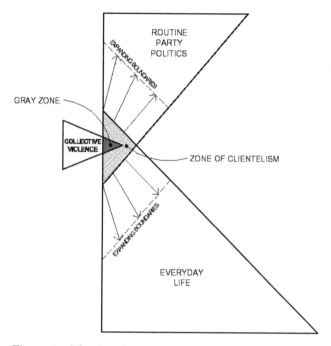

Figure 5. The Gray Zone.

to the poor – not because Peronism has the monopoly over patronage (clientelist politics prevail in Peronism, but Peronism does not own the practice), but because it is there where many of the crucial dimensions of machine politics can be better observed given the party's current control of the national, state, and (a majority of) local government levels.[7] Given their central role during the 2001 lootings at the two sites under investigation, the next chapter pays special attention to one of the key actors in the Peronist machine (i.e., political brokers – some of the most talked-about but least understood actors in contemporary Argentine politics).

---

[7] In their study of a key dimension of clientelist politics (vote buying), Brusco, Nazareno, and Stokes (2004:73) assert that, compared to other parties, the Peronist Party makes the greatest vote-buying effort and displays the greatest effectiveness in these efforts, reflecting "the party's deeper penetration of lower class social networks and hence its greater ability to monitor voters."

Clandestine Connections Count

Everyday life, routine party politics, and collective violence are areas
with their own specific practices, actors, and relations. Figure 5 seeks
to identify the gray zone of intersection between the three areas. It also
illustrates that the boundaries are shifting: The area in which routine
party politics and everyday life overlap is expanding (as we will see in the
next chapter), making patronage politics an increasing presence in the
lives of the poor. The three areas, and their intersections, put in rela-
tion different sets of actors: perpetrators of violence and forces of order
(in the case of collective violence); neighbors, families, and community
leaders (in the case of everyday life); and party leaders and members
(in the case of routine party politics). These are, as becomes clear, analytic distinctions that in real life (and especially in the real life of the
lootings) get blurred. Distinctions between actors get fuzzy, as do what
they are supposed to be doing and how they are supposed (or believed)
to be relating to each other. In this book, I highlight these paradoxical
situations because they aid me in the construction of my explanatory
argument.

The gray zone refers to a set of clandestine connections between
these actors (brokers, repressive forces, residents). This book argues that
concealed, clandestine connections count not only in routine politics
(as the preceding examples illustrate) but also in extraordinary forms of
collective action (such as food riots). This book does not offer a historical
account of the emergence of the gray zone but seeks to scrutinize its
content and form at a particular historical conjuncture. It also shows
how it manifests itself (and with what consequences) in one concrete set
of episodes (i.e., the food lootings). In focusing on *paradoxical* political
occasions (occurrences that are hard or difficult to believe), my account
of the lootings moves from description to explanation (from how to why).
Toward the end of the book, readers might not be able to predict when
the next lootings will happen, but they should be able to know if and when
the episodes actually do take place again, what will have happened earlier
and, maybe, in what specific sequence. If my account of the dynamics of
collective violence is an adequate one, the reader should then be able to

conduct a retrodictive explanation.[8] "Let us imagine a map," Argentine political scientist Guillermo O'Donnell (1993:1359) writes,

> of each country in which the areas covered by blue would designate those where there is a high degree of state presence (in terms of a set of reasonably effective bureaucracies and of the effectiveness of properly sanctioned legality), both functionally and territorially; the green color indicates a high degree of territorial penetration and a significantly lower presence in functional/class terms; and the brown color a very low or nil level in both dimensions.... Brazil and Peru would be dominated by brown, and in Argentina the extensiveness of brown would be smaller – but, if we had a temporal series of maps, we could see that those brown sections have grown lately.

Brown areas, O'Donnell points out, are "neofeudalized regions" where "the obliteration of legality deprives the regional power circuits, including those state agencies, of the public, lawful dimension without which the national state and the order it supports vanish" (1993:1359). In these areas, state organizations become part of a privatized circuit of power; the public dimension of the state evaporates. In these areas, political parties are "personalistic machines" dominated by familism, prebendalism, and/or clientelism. In these areas, finally, we have a "democracy of low-intensity citizenship" (1993:1361). O'Donnell's is not solely a topographic argument; it is also a categorical one.[9] Countries are diversely colored; and the less-advantaged populations are usually the ones that are affected the most:

> [P]easants, slum dwellers, Indians, women, etc. often are unable to receive fair treatment in the courts, or to obtain from state agencies services to which they are entitled, or to be safe from political violence, etc.... [I]n many brown areas the democratic, participatory rights of polyarchy are respected. But the liberal component of democracy is systematically violated. A situation in which one can vote freely and have one's vote counted fairly, but cannot expect proper treatment from the police or the courts, puts in serious question the liberal component of that democracy and severely curtails citizenship. (O'Donnell 1993:1361)

---

[8] In focusing on paradoxes as a criterion to move my descriptions along explanatory lines, I'm following Katz (2001). I'm also borrowing from his understanding of causal explanation as retrodiction.

[9] For an application of O'Donnell's ideas to Brazilian *favela* politics, see Arias (2006).

The Gray Zone

The implications of examining Argentine politics through the lens of the gray zone would be analogous to O'Donnell's cartographic metaphor: The more that routine partisan politics secretly overlap with, on one hand, the organization of violence and, on the other hand, with everyday-life strategies of survival, the more that citizenship and democracy are in danger. Where clandestine relationships prevail, the public dimension of politics is at risk.

The map, however, would look different. As the reader will soon notice, my examples of the gray zone come from the south, the north, and the center of the country; from Cutral-co to Mendoza, from Santiago del Estero to Allen, and from different areas within the Conurbano Bonaerense, from La Matanza to Avellaneda to Moreno: Clandestine connections are everywhere in politics, and the kind of routine politics that analysts recurrently examine (that of parliamentary and electoral politics) is constantly supported by them. Alas, the country's entire map is gray; the categories most implicated in these gray zone practices, however, are those that cover the most vulnerable sectors of the population (the Danis and Jimenas and, as we will soon see, many others who live in poor enclaves or who work close to them).

Coda

The following extended field note was produced – and generously shared – by Argentine sociologist Magdalena Tosoni who is conducting fieldwork in a poor neighborhood located on the west side of the city of Mendoza. The field note provides insightful details as to the existing connections between politics (in this case, community politics) and organized violence (its production and its sometimes-negotiated avoidance). The field note also shows in situ the codes used by some actors to speak about their links to the criminal underworld and the difficulties that those without those connections have in understanding such codified ways of talking and acting.

Voluntary Help

In early 2004, the neighborhood association of "El Alamito" begins to seek state funding to organize an after-school program and a soup kitchen. Juan, the president, invites local teacher Mariela to join the program. Mariela gladly accepts and begins registering neighborhood children. Soon, she becomes the visible face of the after-school program. Beto regularly attends the meetings of the neighborhood association. He is a friend of the president and very famous in the barrio (he's been in jail twice). When he finds out about the proposed program, he registers his two sons and pledges to find more teachers to support his friend the president's initiative.

While the neighborhood association is waiting for the state funds to start the project, meetings are organized with the mothers of the children who will be attending the after-school program. The idea is to get their help to organize the soup kitchen. At one of those meetings, Mariela meets Beto. When the meeting is over, Beto asks Mariela about the starting date of the program and offers his "help." The following is the dialogue that ensues:

BETO: So, when are you starting?

MARIELA: We are waiting for the subsidy from the government. Next week we have a meeting in the municipal building. I'm pretty sure it's going to start in April.

BETO: I told Juan that I'm going to help. I told him to let me know when the program begins so that I can talk to the guys here, so that they don't bother you.

MARIELA (without understanding): Ah . . .

BETO: I can help with the after-school program in that way. I know [the guys], but I need you to tell me [about the starting date] well in advance. I have to stay here overnight and talk to them.

MARIELA: OK, I'll let you know . . .

After a month, at another meeting, Beto and Mariela meet again.

MARIELA: I think we are going to start in June. We are waiting for the funds so that we can buy chairs, tables, buy some stationery for the kids, pencils, notebooks . . .

BETO: You already know that I want to help. I know the kids here in the neighborhood very well. I'll tell them not to bother you, to let you work... because you know how things are these days in the neighborhood.

MARIELA: Are you saying that because of what Juan said the other day about the robberies and the threats to that local family?

BETO: Yes. Here there's a struggle going on to see who's going to be the new boss.

MARIELA: Are they seeing who's the strongest?

BETO: Yes, something like that. That's why I'm saying that I can be of help, talk to the kids, but I need to know when you are starting [with the program]. I'll stay overnight, talk to them, but I need to spend the whole night, chatting.... I know how these things are, I know people who are in prison, you know I've been inside. I also know people in the police; I know how these things work.

MARIELA: Yes (doubting)...well...OK...I'll let you know.

BETO: I already told Juan that I can help.

In August, the neighborhood association opens the soup kitchen and the after-school program. As they are finishing their day, Mariela tells Susana [cousin of Beto's girlfriend, new worker in the program, hired at the recommendation of Beto] that they should get ready ["organize"] to leave. Susana should lock the doors, while she, Mariela, takes the keys to the president's house. They would then leave together. Susana answers:

SUSANA: I have no problems [leaving]. Beto already talked to the people. They won't do anything to us.

MARIELA (with surprise all over her face): OK, so...he talked to the neighborhood groups.

SUSANA: Yes, yes...and I'm relaxed.

MARIELA (looking amazed): ... [long silence]

2

Party Politics and Everyday Life

During the 1990s, the Peronist Party shifted its urban organization from union to clientelist networks (Levitsky and Murillo 2006; Levitsky 2003). The mutually reinforcing processes of state-retrenchment, hyperunemployment, and mass-immiseration (Auyero 2000) substantially increased the influence of local brokers and party bosses who provide access to scarce state resources. As Brusco, Nazareno, and Stokes (2004:67) assert, "the recent shift to pro-market policies and the downsizing of the state seem not to have eliminated political clientelism, contrary to some expectations.... Neoliberalism may have revived clientelism." Patronage politics is hardly new in Argentina (Rock 2005), but its social, political, and cultural relevance has escalated since the early 1990s – coincidentally, at the time when radical neoliberal reforms were undertaken by the Menem administration. During the 1990s and 2000s, as O'Donnell's (1993) "brown areas" increase their relevance in Argentina's social and political landscape, we witness the consolidation of this political practice.

Manolo and the Seventy-Five Buses

Manuel Quindimil has been the mayor of Lanús, a municipality located in Greater Buenos Aires, for the last twenty years. He is, according to the slogan of the last electoral campaign, "the last *caudillo*" (this slogan has been reiterated during, at least to my knowledge, the last decade). During the last presidential elections (2003), Manolo sent seventy-five buses loaded with his followers to the main rally organized by the current president Néstor Kirchner in the River Plate soccer stadium. Below is an edited description of the day of the rally and of the dominant political practices in the district as seen by a foreign observer:

> Estela Cabrera, who lives in a shantytown [in Lanús], attended [the rally]. With Argentines set to vote for a new president this Sunday, such rallies – with their massive banners and loud drums – are an everyday part of life here, especially for shantytown residents such as Cabrera. Cabrera, a mother of 11, is separated from her husband and has, for the past five years, been unemployed. But she is a busy woman. She cares for her youngsters, works 20 hours a week in a nearby soup kitchen to earn a monthly unemployment subsidy and, until the early morning hours, knits pullovers for less than a dollar each, allowing herself only five hours' rest before her hectic day begins again.... Cabrera did not know which candidate she would be rallying for, just that she would be showing up. A few days before the rally, Cabrera said that she would attend only because the manager of her soup kitchen would cut her from the workfare rolls if she did not. "You have to go, no matter what," Cabrera explained. To her, the rally would be just like any day of work. "If I miss the rally, I need to bring a medical certificate saying I'm sick or that one of my kids is sick," she said, resigned and exasperated at the same time. "Even if I were sick, where would I get a medical certificate from?" María Coronel [is] the administrator of soup kitchens in Lanús.... In her municipal office, Coronel told me that none of the soup-kitchen managers are involved in politics or mobilize people for rallies. "If any do, I don't know about it," she said. But Coronel was being less than truthful. For the Kirchner rally, Coronel herself badgered managers into pledging to fill 40 buses; meanwhile, a smaller set of managers especially faithful to Coronel promised to bring 12 busloads of her people from her territory. Coronel's political base is the "Happy Children" soup kitchen, where more than 100 people, including me, assembled for the rally. We rode to the stadium on buses displaying Coronel's name in the front window.... [Most of the people in the bus] work at Coronel's soup kitchen as workfare recipients, have children that eat at a Coronel-affiliated soup kitchen or eat there themselves.... [Most of them] including Cabrera, did not know the purpose of the rally....

Manolo has achieved near-dictatorial social and political control of Lanús by channeling state resources to the poor almost exclusively through his network of brokers. Every aid program in Lanús is run largely through the brokers – from the national workfare program to the provincial "Glass of Milk" and foodstuff-distribution programs to municipal services, such as after-school help, primary-assistance medical care, and karate and yoga classes.[1]

What's going on here? The story of Manolo, Estela, and María vivifies the hoarding of state resources by political brokers and patrons of the Peronist Party that we saw expressed in the complaints of Jimena and Daniel in the previous chapter. In what follows, I scrutinize the workings of the Peronist network among the urban poor in both its material and symbolic dimensions. This examination is not meant to provide a complete account of the Peronist way of doing politics among the urban poor but to highlight certain aspects of what is commonly known as "Peronist clientelism" that are deemed important to understand the overlap between the everyday life of those living in destitute neighborhoods and the daily operation of the Peronist Party – understanding that is crucial to comprehend the lootings' dynamics.[2]

The empirical argument of this chapter runs as follows: Taking advantage of their privileged position, brokers from the Peronist Party sequester state resources with which they (a) solve poor people's everyday problems, (b) accumulate political capital that helps them advance in the political field, and (c) maintain the Peronist machine in a working state. In solving poor people's problems on a daily basis through individual transactions, brokers establish social ties with their clients. These ties, after repeated iterations, concatenate into networks that link patrons, brokers, and the urban poor. At a more analytical level, this chapter identifies a set of practices the sheer existence of which collapses easily and simplifying (but still widespread) distinctions between state and nonstate institutions, formal and informal politics, everyday life and electoral politics. State, partisan routine politics, and daily life are seen as analytically separable spheres that, in real life, are mutually imbricated.

---

[1] From Goldberg (2003c).

[2] In this chapter, I revisit arguments I made in *Poor People's Politics* (2001). This is an analytic revisit [not an ethnographic one; see Burawoy 2003] in that I did not go back to my previous field site (Villa Paraíso). This chapter adds new material to support or qualify the claims made in that earlier work. The new material was culled from fieldwork in two districts of Buenos Aires (Avellaneda and Moreno), in Santiago del Estero, and from secondary sources [mainly newspaper accounts and investigative reports but also some scholarly accounts (Grimson et al. 2004; Levitsky 2003; Torres 2002)].

Hoarding

> Whatever its specific historical origins, the political machine persists as an apparatus for satisfying otherwise unfulfilled needs of diverse groups in the population. Robert K. Merton, *Social Theory and Social Structure.*

> April 2003. In a shantytown called Hope, in a municipality that borders Argentina's capital city, armed teenagers stand on street corners, charging "tolls" of passersby and dealing drugs. It is a scene out of the movie *City of God.* The shantytown's name aside, hope here is elusive. But Marta Belisan, a Peronist broker in the shantytown, provides an oasis of optimism from her expansive, sturdy shack, which serves as both her home and a soup kitchen. On the day I visited Belisan, three large trucks – which together make up the mobile hospital of Lanús – were parked outside her residence. A long line of mothers and screaming children were waiting to be seen. Belisan is part of the mayor's network of neighborhood problem solvers. She provides help to the most desperate, and if, in return, Hope residents have to attend a few rallies for presidential candidate Néstor Kirchner – one of four major contenders in this Sunday's presidential election [and currently the President of Argentina] – they are often eager to do so.... Residents of shantytowns have a lot of problems: they need to find food for themselves and their children; they need free medication or burial services; they need plastic sheets to build a new shack because a kerosene stove exploded, burning down the shack they had worked years to assemble from wood scraps. There are also a lot of things they would like to have, such as pipes to install a sewer system (so their children stop getting parasitic infections, which are endemic especially where shantytowns have been built over swamps).... Belisan the broker is available, like most *punteros*, at any hour of the day or night. Her activities vary from obtaining identification documents from the municipality to throwing a pizza birthday party for a 71-year old man without a family to trucking out the body of a young boy so ravaged by a dog that the municipal health service refused to remove it, according to locals.[3]

Foreign correspondent Jonathan Goldberg is rightly pointing at a widespread yet still little-explored political practice in contemporary Argentina. With unemployment hovering around 14 to 16 percent, and more than half of Argentines living below the official poverty line, poor people find in brokers of the Peronist Party one of the few outlets to satisfy their basic material needs. As Goldberg's account highlights,

[3] From Goldberg (2003b).

Peronist brokers are deeply embedded in the everyday life of the destitute in Argentina.

Let me briefly outline the form and function of Peronist problem-solving networks (for a detailed account, see Auyero 2001). In poor and working-class neighborhoods, shantytowns, and squatter settlements throughout the country, many of the poor and the unemployed solve the pressing problems of everyday life (access to food and medicine, for example) through patronage networks that rely on brokers of the Peronist Party (locally known as *punteros*) as key actors (see also Levitsky 2003; Torres 2002). Depending on the (not always legal, not always overt) support of the local, provincial, and national administrations, these problem-solving networks work as webs of resource distribution and of protection against the risks of everyday life. *Punteros* provide food in state-funded soup kitchens; broker access to state subsidies for the unemployed or to public hospitals; distribute food and/or food vouchers to mothers, children, and the elderly; and occasionally give out toys (manufactured by workfare recipients) to parents who cannot afford such items. As Goldberg (2003a:3) writes: "The main source for all these most basic necessities [food, clothes, and medicine] among impoverished Argentines is the Peronist neighborhood broker, or *puntero*." Other basic needs aside, the procurement of food is, according to my own ethnographic work and those of other analysts (Torres 2002; Levitsky 2003; Goldberg 2003a, 2003b; Grimson et al. 2004), the main task of brokers of the Peronist Party. Steve Levitsky's (2003) recent work on the transformation of the Peronist Party provides an exhaustive examination of the PJ (Partido Justicialista) activities. Based on a survey of 112 UBs (Unidades Básicas – grassroots offices of the Peronist Party) in La Matanza, Quilmes, and the Federal Capital, Levitsky (2003:188) shows that more than two-thirds of them engage in direct distribution of food or medicine. Nearly a quarter of them regularly provide jobs for their constituents. Sixty percent of the UBs of Greater Buenos Aires surveyed by this author participate in the implementation of at least one government social program. In another recent study of three Argentine provinces (Buenos Aires, Córdoba, and Misiones), Brusco, Nazareno, and Stokes found that 44 percent of the 1,920 respondents "reported that parties gave things out to individuals in their neighborhood during the campaign. The most common item respondents mentioned was food, but they also mentioned clothing, mattresses, medicine, milk, corrugated metal, construction materials, blankets, hangers, utility bill payments, money, eyeglasses, chickens, trees, and magnets" (2004:69). This recent survey shows in unambiguous terms the extent of clientelist practices among the poor:

> [M]ore than one-third of [the] full sample (and 45 percent of low-income respondents) would turn to a party operative [a *puntero*] for help if the head of his or her household lost their job.... [M]ore than one in five low-income voters had turned to a political patron for help in the previous year ... 12 percent of poor voters – 18 percent of poor voters who sympathized with the Peronist Party – acknowledged having received a handout from a party operative in the 2001 campaign. (2004:69)

In Lomas Verde, Moreno, where part of my research on the lootings took place, two of the most important brokers have housing cooperatives, distribute milk for a state-sponsored program, and manage the largest soup kitchen in the area.

Brokers direct flows of goods, information, and services from their political patrons to their clients and flows of political support (in the form of attendance at rallies, participation in party activities, and sometimes votes) from their clients to their patrons. Being members of the governing Peronist Party, they have the personal connections that enable them to gain access to resources and information about them. Brokers know the whens, hows, and wheres of the allocation of welfare resources (from distribution of foodstuffs to the spread of information concerning a new program) and continuously attempt to position themselves as the only channels that facilitate transactions or resource flows.

> "What are you doing here? You are no longer in the program," said a Peronist *puntero* to Alejandra, a 34-year-old unemployed woman, who was about to claim her unemployment subsidy at the local branch of the state bank in Lanús. At the local municipality, officials had informed her that she was on the list of entitled recipients. At the bank, however, an employee told her that another woman, who happened to be the *puntero's* wife, had claimed the subsidy under her name with a note which, including Alejandra's personal information, asserted that "she was unable to attend." (Irina Hauser, "Los peajes del Plan Jefas," *Página 12 Digital*, Web-accessed January 14, 2004)

The preceding story, thoughtfully entitled "The tolls of the Plan Jefas," describes one of the instances in which part of the resources of the largest welfare program in Argentina (the *Plan Jefas y Jefes* to which Daniel and Jimena refer in the previous chapter) ends up in the hands of Peronist brokers. This particular program has become, in the last year, the mainstay of subsistence for 1.8 million unemployed who receive a cash subsidy of $150 (U.S.$50) every month. In exchange, they have to perform four to six hours of work daily – carrying out community work, attending school, and so on. Funded by the national treasury, new taxes on exports, and a loan of U.S.$600 million from the World Bank, the program is similar to *and* different from previous "social programs" in Argentina: It is different in its magnitude (it is the largest welfare program, so far, covering close to 20 percent of Argentine households), in the amount of legal regulations that govern it, and in the rhetorical framing that emphasizes an unspecified "right to social inclusion." It is similar in that it puts emphasis on "assistance" to those in need (rather than on income redistribution) and in that, if we are to believe the evidence culled by journalists, human rights advocates, and some state agencies, it ends up financing part of the operation of the Peronist machine through the "tolls" that brokers collect for granting access to the program (see CELS 2003). Crucial in this respect is the fact that, after much wrestling involving federal and local officials, mayors kept control of the on-the-ground administration of the program. Mayors throughout the country have de facto veto power regarding who is and who is not a welfare recipient. Similar to other welfare programs (now extinct or still in operation, like *Plan Vida*, the *Bono Solidario*, the *Planes Trabajar*, and the *Programa de Emerencia Laboral*), the *Jefas y Jefes* turns into one key state resource that circulates within the Peronist problem-solving network and oils the operation of the Peronist machine.

Dominating

The more we hang around poverty enclaves, the closer we look at what brokers, patrons, and clients of the Peronist machine do on the ground, on a daily basis, and the clearer becomes our view of the daily construction of Peronist domination. Brokers and patrons of the Peronist Party pursue their own political careers, try to accumulate as much political power as they can, and improve their positions in the local political field. In order to do so, they attempt to maximize their intake of state resources (material goods distributed by the state, welfare programs, and information) vital to solving poor people's problems *and* to winning followers: They do politics through problem solving. They surely do not directly command the actions of poor people who need to solve pressing survival needs. Yet, the structural domination effects that are entailed in the position of Peronist brokers should be clear. In pursuing their own interests (improving their positions in the local political field through the accumulation of political capital), some of them achieve a quasi-monopoly on problem solving.[4] In so doing, they increase their capacity to narrow and constrain the possibilities of problem-holders (i.e., they dominate).

Social scientist Karina Mallamaci's (2003) detailed study of educational policy making and implementation in Lomas de Zamora (a district in the Conurbano governed by Peronism until 1999) offers evidence of the practical convergence between actors within the school system (principals and teachers) and actors within the clientelist network (brokers and clients) while pointing at the politicization (i.e., organization along party lines) of otherwise presumed nonparty organizations: the COCs (Center of Community Organization), the Educational Council (Consejo Escolar), and two nongovernmental organizations. Her study also detects that "neighborhood health units, local daycares, and even schools establish specific [exchange] relationships with the local [party] problem-solving network." She writes (2003:50–1):

> Twelve of the nineteen observed schools obtained goods or services through contacts with local politicians: [they got] their lawn mowed, sausages, bread, and drinks for a festival, a bus to drive students back to their homes, an entertainment center, fans for a classroom, paint for the building, the expansion of the state-funded milk program for the school, medicine for kids' lice infection. For the politicians involved in these transactions, they imply a good opportunity to deploy their party strategies. Although they obtain concrete benefits, schools can also be losing

---

[4] This process is not devoid of struggle as even a superficial look at the factionalism within the PJ will attest.

others if the competition between politicians is strong – two competing politicians will not benefit a school population that is already the clientele of someone else.

The evidence regarding the actual capacity of PJ patronage for getting votes is quite mixed (for contradictory evidence, see Auyero 2001; Brusco, Nazareno, and Stokes 2004; Calvo and Murillo 2004). What is undeniable is that the very workings of the networks help the Peronist Party to solve important organizational problems: funding the party's operational costs, maintaining the party in an active state between elections, providing crucial personnel during primaries and general elections, and so on. Favors are given (bags of food, medicines, speedy access to a welfare plan, etc.) and reciprocated with rally attendance, voting in primary elections, shows of support, and the like. Brokers test, in practice, the allegiance of their followers, while clients experience, again in practice, the reliability of brokers and patrons.

Unsubtle Modes

In 2002, the main newspaper of Santiago del Estero published an investigative report entitled "The Foundations of Power." In the cover photo, there are two bricks, with the names of the then-governor Juarez and his wife Nina printed on them. The bricks, the report asserts, were used to build public housing. Santiago del Estero is probably one of the most obvious examples of patronage and clientelist politics in contemporary Argentina (see Auyero 2003). The report details some of the ways in which corruption and clientelism, although analytically separable, go together in everyday political practice. The report also shows one way (not very subtle, if compared to others) in which parties and local governments attempt to build political loyalty.

"I'd like to ask you to replace Mr. Luis Cejas... – following legal procedures if at all possible – with the lady who has been the secretary of the Unidad Básica, and who has been with us for a long time and we haven't given her anything and she also has seven children. Her name is Teresa Tévez." This is the text of a memo signed by Yolanda Quiroga de Cisterna, a member of the Women's Branch of the Peronist Party for the neighborhood of Sarmiento. The memo was sent to Mr. Rizzo Patrón, current vice-chief in the Secretary of Emergency Plans.... This was not the only memo. We were able to obtain many documents that...reflect the power that Peronist activists have in the Institute of Housing and Urbanism [*Instituto Provincial de la Vivienda y Urbanismo*]. According to regulations, the supervision should be carried out by social workers that are employed in that area. But members of the Peronist Women's Branch won't allow them to do their job [*El despliegue de la Rama Femenina las deja postradas en las oficinas del Instituto, sin nada que hacer*]. The Peronist Women's Branch and other Peronist groups...apparently have a quota of houses that they directly give out. Many sources in the Institute told us so. According to these sources, the Institute distributes at most "15% of the houses."

"I, Jugo Manuel (general secretary of the Unidad Básica 8 de Abril), report that...Manuela Santillán gives up her benefits [from the social welfare program called *Plan de Ayuda Mutua*]. It is proposed that Jugo Manuel takes her place." That means Jugo Manuel proposes himself as a new beneficiary.... For many years now, Juarismo made housing one of the pillars of their social policy. The idea is quite clear: hammer into people's heads the idea that the government is the one giving the house as a gift, even when the beneficiary has to pay for it in installments. "To be honest, we don't care much if we don't get the money back," says an employee of the Institute. "It is anti-political, because it is expected that people think that the governor himself is the one bestowing the house." (From *Informe Especial I "Los Cimientos del Poder," El Liberal, Santiago del Estero, 2001*)

Veiling

> We might coin the term common miscognition to designate this game in which everyone knows – and does not want to know – that everyone knows – and those who not want to know – the true nature of exchanges.
> Pierre Bourdieu, *Pascalian Meditations*

[Marta] Belisan...categorically denies that the state services she provides are related to her political activities for the mayor. "We don't ask people, 'Can you come to the rally?' We tell them, 'Do you want to come to the rally?'" Belisan says. "The mayor doesn't like politics and social action to be mixed." But as Elsira Ramirez explains, her job – rounding up Belisan's clients when there is a rally – is an easy one, seeing as "the people already know us." Everyone in Hope knows Belisan and her inner circle.... An elderly woman who plays cards in the afternoon in the soup kitchen explains why she boards Belisan's buses. "She's got the [workfare] plans that are given out here," the woman says. "She's got medication, she's got things for here." (From "Client Privilege," Jonathan Goldberg, American Prospect Web site, April 2003, accessed August 2003)

Such denial of the demand for votes and support in exchange for favors and goods is hardly the lone work of the Martas who labor in municipal offices throughout Argentina. It is part of what Bourdieu calls "collective denial," a symbolic dimension that is constitutive of the operation of Peronist machine politics.[5] Sometimes, recipients like Estela Cabrera are "resigned and exasperated" about the strings attached to the goods delivered by the broker. "*Soguero*" – a term we first heard in La Matanza to describe a powerful local broker – is the term that better encapsulates this critical view of brokers: "*Soguero*" refers to someone who throws you a rope (*soga*), someone who gives you a hand. The meaning of "*soguero*" does not stop there: That same rope (or that same hand, for that matter), in turn, can be used to strangle you. In years studying clientelism, I never heard a term that better synthesizes the dualism of brokerage: problem solving and naked domination.

But that is hardly the whole story about Peronist machine politics. Many other times, recipients of brokers' patronage, especially those with long-lasting ties with their benefactors, see them as "friends," "caring neighbors," or "good people" and think and feel that partisan problem solving is not their "right" but a "favor" performed by helpful and responsible people. Sometimes, as in the case of Santiago del Estero described earlier, patronage works seemingly in the open; at other times, patronage is veiled in subtle and deceiving ways. The following two sets of conversations that I had with shantytown dwellers attest to this diversity.

A conversation about destitution and clientelism in a shantytown in the outskirts of Buenos Aires follows:

TOMÁS: Look, there go the buses to pick people up...

JAVIER: And people go?

---

[5] For a full exploration of this dimension of patronage, see Auyero (2001).

TOMÁS: Yes, people go . . . I don't get it . . . I swear, I don't get it . . .

TOMÁS: They use them . . .

JAVIER: And don't they realize they are being used?

TOMÁS: People are too obsequious (*obsecuente*) . . . or there's too much misery. Maybe they have hopes that they are going to get some help . . .

SILVIA (block delegate working for the welfare program *Plan Vida*[6]): I tell my husband that we should be thankful when people do you a favor. Andrea [municipal official and local broker] told me: "The only favor I'll ask you is that you come with me to the rallies." And I told her: "Sure, no problem." My husband sometimes doesn't allow me to go because there might be trouble. . . . But I tell him that thanks to Andrea we have the pension. I made the effort, because every time they told me to go to a rally I went, so that they could see that I was interested, because if someone doesn't budge, doesn't show interest . . .

JAVIER: And how did you get elected to be a block delegate for the *Plan Vida*?

SILVIA: Well, it was also because of Andrea. She got us involved. One day she came and told me about this, but I didn't quite understand because it was the first time. . . . One gives help and we help each other.

Moral indictments made by well-intentioned journalists (Di Natale 2005) and by analysts who focus on the collective actors that have organized in opposition to machine-clientelist politics[7] would have us believe that the dominant practice within the specific social universe of Peronist problem-solving networks is that of explicit commands made by brokers to their clients every time they hand out the goods. Machine politics, for its critics, is all about plain orders and material resources. The more goods and services patrons and brokers distribute, the more the support they get and the more power they have. Hoarding and domination, however, do not live a single life in the objectivity of resource distribution. Paraphrasing Bourdieu, we should point out that the network lives another life in the dispositions it inculcates in some of its

---

[6] *Plan Vida* is the name of a welfare program that distributes milk, cereal, and eggs to needy pregnant women and children.

[7] Such as the recent *piquetero* movement (i.e., the movement of jobless workers).

actors – dispositions that ensure the reproduction of this arrangement. The automatic appearance of the exchange of "support for favors" should not be interpreted in mechanistic terms but as the result of the habituation it generates in beneficiaries or clients. The *everyday* working of problem-solving networks infuses in those who receive the daily favors from patrons and brokers a set of dispositions (and I emphasize the regular, routine operation of the network to highlight that this *relationship* of exchange transcends singular acts of exchange). These schemes of perception, evaluation, and action are, in turn, reconfirmed by the symbolic actions that patrons and brokers routinely enact in their public speeches (emphasizing the "love" they feel for their followers and their "service to the people") and in their personalized ways of giving (stressing *their* efforts to obtain the goods and thus creating the appearance that were they not there, the benefits would not be delivered).

The network inscribes the relations of domination in the minds of beneficiaries-turned-into-followers, in the form of durable dispositions – evidenced in the innumerable manifestations of respect ("I think he [the broker] should be recognized for all what he is doing for the neighbors"), admiration ("[T]he way he takes care of people, he is an exceptional human being"), and even friendship ("We consider ourselves her friend," "She is always present when something happens.... She is so good," "She pays attention to every single detail") that clients sometimes discursively articulate about their benefactors. Most of the time, however, these dispositions manifest *in practice* through the things party clients simply *know* ("I tell my husband we have to be thankful ...," "Because she gave me medicine, or some milk, or a packet of yerba or sugar, I *know* that I have to go to her rally in order to fulfill my obligation to her, to show my gratitude"). Acts of knowledge are, we are reminded by this last testimony, acts of submission.

To be blunt, patronage might be based on material resources, but it has a crucial symbolic dimension that is entirely missed by most analysts who repeatedly predict a looming "crisis of machine politics" (a "crisis," I should add, that has presumably been in the making for a decade now). The daily social order of the machine has durable effects via the dispositions it instills in clients' beliefs. The authority of specific patrons and brokers might well come from the resources they wield, but the authority of machine politics and the authority of brokers and patrons in general come from habituation to the everyday workings of the network. In the daily workings of patronage what matters most are not short-term quid-pro-quo exchanges but diffuse, long-term reciprocity, based on the embedding of the machine operators (brokers and, through them, patrons) in poor people's everyday lives.

Segundo Alberto Herrera is 58 years old and the president of the Retirees Club in BID, La Matanza. He has been involved in local party politics until quite recently. We interviewed him at length in June 2005. The following excerpt captures the symbolic dimension of clientelism (from the broker's viewpoint) quite well, a dimension that analysts concerned with the immorality (and/or illegality) of this kind of political practice routinely dismiss or ignore:

> I was working in the political campaign to elect [current mayor] Balestrini. I had 21 Unidades Básicas. When we had to go to a rally, I called my people, and ten buses were never enough, because I filled them up. And never, never in my life, did I pay people to attend rallies. They went to the rally to be with me (*para acompañarme*), not for a bottle of wine or anything.... When Balestrini won, I organized a big party. Mind you, I had not been elected or anything. I spoke and told those who had been with me that I was thankful for all the times they went with me to the rallies. After each rally, as they were coming out of the buses, I thanked them for coming. And they asked me: "Why are you thanking us if we are doing this from the bottom of our hearts [*lo hacemos de corazón*]?" I had a big following when I was working in politics.

Close-up, on-the-ground observation of problem solvers and problem holders in real time and space shows us people receiving goods, obtaining access to various state programs through personal contacts, attending rallies, voting in primary elections, and committing themselves to daily party work. Different forms of social interaction take place within this specific social universe. Everyday trips to the Unidad Básica, routine rounds to the Municipality, endless meetings with brokers and party gatherings constitute a realm of sociability with its own rules, its catalog of things to say and not to say, to do and not to do, with its own taken-for-grantedness, its own doxa. Ethnography also provides us with evidence concerning the collective denial of any sort of quid pro quo; a subjective, but hardly individual, refutation of the objective exchange. To what end? True, this collective denial humanizes and personalizes the assistance given to those in need (Merton 1949) – a dimension not to be underestimated in a context, such as Argentina, in which official neglect and indifference toward the plight of poor people have long prevailed – but it also masks the unequal balance of power within this hierarchical arrangement, presenting resource-hoarding as a "service to the people."

CODA 1: Mabel in Moreno

Mabel has lived in Lomas Verde, in the district of Moreno, since 1985. Her husband works in a bakery in nearby Villa Ballester. Together they have seven children, six of them still living in their household. Mabel is an active member of the local Peronist party. She directs the soup kitchen *Por los Pibes* (For the Kids) with funds from the local, state, and federal governments. *Por los Pibes* serves 290 beneficiaries, and some of them have their lunches in premises that Mabel built with the help of the municipal government. Others pick up their food and have lunch at home. Eleven beneficiaries of the *Plan Jefas y Jefes* work in the soup kitchen under Mabel's supervision. She first coordinated a soup kitchen (not a *comedor* as she does now, but a less organized *olla popular*) in the late 1980s under Alfonsín's presidency. As she told us: "My niece was not doing well, and she asked me if I could get milk for her . . . I went to the municipality and they offered me help to get a soup-kitchen started." Soon, she was involved in many other welfare programs (the provincial *copa de leche* program being one) and became the vice-president of the local improvement association (*Sociedad de Fomento*). "I've been in politics for years," Mabel tells me. And for her, politics means, as for many others, attending to poor neighbors' needs, helping them on a daily basis. In return, she gets recognition and support from them that eventually translate into good standing in the party and more resources for her, resources that further her political work. "I'm everywhere . . . any problem [that neighbors have], they all come to see me," she proudly tells me. "But I can't solve every single problem! People keep demanding and demanding." When there are elections, she says, "I gave my people the ballots to vote for the person I tell them to ... they know what to do."

CODA 2: Brokers and Activism

Members of two different unemployed workers organizations [*Movimiento de Trabajadores Desocupados* (MTDs)] told the following stories to Marina Sitrin (2005:126–8). The stories speak not only of the persistence of patronage but also of its (perceived) pernicious effects on popular community activism:

> Right now we are between 500 and 600 people who are actively involved every week. At first, in the first meetings [*asambleas*], I remember we were 300 from the neighborhood. We then began to grow and were 400, then 500, and then around 1000, or a little more than 1000. Generally during the electoral campaigns, there was a drop in participation in the movement. This is because the political machines put a lot of money into buying people, and because of that the movements suffer a decrease. I remember in the neighborhoods, in the last campaign, they tried to buy people who were the most involved and engaged in the movement, and they offered them a lot of money. For example the sister, who is active in the movement, was telling us about a person who worked for the government ... they [people in the government] would give her a lot of money if she was able to buy off a piquetero, a piquetero was more expensive, so to speak, because they were fighting. They offered a lot of money as well as goods and stuff. It is difficult [to struggle against that, because], for example, they offered a salary of $1500. (Solano, MTD member)

> We are coming from a drop in the number of people involved in the movement, a decrease. I believe that it has a lot to do with the electoral question. The electoral process sucks up a lot of *compañeros*. They go to the municipality and work for a campaign. What it looks like is that politicians come to the neighborhoods and throw

a huge quantity of pesos at *compañeros* to try and buy them, including people that are really valued, like, for example, in the case of Verónica, a *compañera* that had developed a lot in the movement... [people who were able to] talk in the name of the movement in front of a mobilization of maybe 14–15 thousand people. Can you imagine the degree of political development in order to do this [to speak in front of a huge crowd]? When she talked, everybody went silent [*no soplaba una mosca*]. There is so much time and energy [devoted to] political development... and then the elections come and some *compañeros* are bought by the municipality to work for the party. And that is how such a large number of *compañeros* left, so many *compañeros*. In this way, due to the electoral campaigns, we have lost not only the *compañeros* but also the unemployment subsidies that belong to them. (Allen, MTD member)

3

Food Lootings

Argentine Lootings 1989–1990

The first food riots in modern Argentina began on May 25, 1989, in the provinces of Córdoba and Rosario, and by May 30, when a state of siege was declared by the federal government, lootings exploded in the Conurbano Bonaerense. Described by newspapers as poor, humble residents of peripheral neighborhoods, hundreds of looters broke into food markets shouting, "Cut prices, we are hungry!" By June 6, massive lootings had taken place in Buenos Aires, Mendoza, and Tucumán, and smaller episodes occurred in Corrientes, San Juan, and Santiago del Estero; fourteen people were dead, almost a hundred were injured, and four hundred had been arrested throughout the country. The geography of death and injury closely correlates with the intensity of the episodes: Seven were killed in Buenos Aires, mainly in the "hot zones" of the Conurbano – as local newspapers called Moreno, San Miguel, General Sarmiento, Ciudadela, and Morón (i.e., the western area of Greater Buenos Aires) – with more isolated episodes in the south (i.e., Quilmes, Lanús, and Avellaneda), six in Rosario and Villa Gobernador Galvez, and one in Tucumán. The lootings occurred in the context of an unprecedented hyperinflationary crisis (during the first five months of 1989, prices of staple foods rose between 400 and 1000 percent, while wages increased 200 percent over a year) and of sudden massive cutbacks in the main national food distribution program (*Programa de Alimentación Nacional*) (Prevot-Schapira 1993:790). Violence and repression increased rapidly during the first week. According to Serul-nikov (1994:71),

> [a]t the beginning, the actions were carried out by small groups composed principally of women. They came into the stores peacefully, filled their bags and shopping carts with milk, sugar, rice, flour, and other basic foods, and then left without paying. Outside, people helped them carry away the stolen food. At no time did they attempt to steal money from the cash registers.

As lootings diffused and government repression stepped up, newspapers reported more violent assaults, which included stores other than food markets (appliances, electronics, clothing). Lootings subsided after the first week of June but returned briefly by mid-July in Rosario, Tucumán, and Córdoba. Despite the official rhetoric that pointed to "subversive agitators" as the organizers of the riots, no evidence was found regarding their presence.

Most Argentines know about the major outcome of the lootings: They precipitated the scheduled inauguration of President-elect Menem. The food riots also provoked the immediate freezing of basic food prices and the reestablishment of government food subsidies (Serulnikov 1994:70). Eight months later, between February 20 and 25, 1990, a shorter, less intense, more geographically focused, and nonfatal wave of lootings shook the beginning of Menem's presidency but was quickly quelled by the combined efforts of state and federal police.

Much like other major riots in Bolivia (2003) and Venezuela (1989), the lootings in Argentina triggered major political changes. As said, in 1989 the first wave of massive lootings occurred during a dramatic hyperinflationary crisis and speeded up the transfer of office from President Alfonsín to President Menem. In 2001, widespread food lootings together with massive *cacerolazos* determined the end of President De La Rua's administration.

Argentine Lootings 2001

> Grievances are fundamental to rebellion as oxygen is fundamental to combustion. But just as fluctuations in the oxygen content of the air account for little of the distribution of fire in the workaday world, fluctuations in

grievances are not a major cause of the presence or absence of rebellion. For that, the political means of acting on grievances which people have at their disposal matter a good deal more.

Charles Tilly (Town and Country in Revolution)

On the morning of December 14, 2001, the cities of Rosario (in the central province of Santa Fe) and Concordia (in the eastern province of Entre Ríos) witnessed the first groups of poor people gathering in front of supermarkets demanding food. When denied, they began breaking into the premises and taking away merchandise while store owners, managers, and employees looked on in bewildered disbelief, and policemen, if they reach the stores in time, attempted to prevent further looting. During the next few days, the sacking of grocery stores and supermarkets extended unevenly throughout the country, and by the end of the week of December 14–22, a series of such episodes had occurred in 11 Argentine states. Maps 1 and 2 describe the initial progress of looting throughout the country on December 14 and 15. Map 3 shows the geographic distribution of the total amount of lootings from December 14 to 22.

By the week's end, eighteen people (all of them under 35 years old) had been killed either by the police or by store owners. Hundreds more were seriously injured, and thousands were arrested. The states of Santa Fe, Entre Ríos, and Mendoza and the districts of Avellaneda and Quilmes in the state of Buenos Aires were the first to experience the uprisings – hundreds of persons blockading roads, publicly demanding food, and eventually looting stores and markets. Yet the violence soon extended unevenly to the south, center, and north of the country reaching the highly populated and urbanized state of Córdoba and spreading rapidly though unevenly throughout Buenos Aires. Interestingly, the poorest and most unequal states in the northeast and the northwest reported no looting activity. Similarly, some of the poorest districts in Buenos Aires (Florencio Varela, for example) suffered no looting.

Although spectacular in their intensity and extent, the lootings were hardly isolated moments of collective violence in Argentina. They were part of what social movement scholarship would call a "cycle of collective action" (Tarrow 1998). During the past two decades, new and unconventional forms of popular contention transformed Argentina into a

Map 1. The Geographic Distribution of Lootings, December 14, 2001. Map created by the Laboratorio de Sistemas de Información Geográfica (Universidad Nacional de General Sarminent) on the basis of author's data.

Map 2. The Geographic Distribution of Lootings, December 15, 2001. Map created by the Laboratorio de Sistemas de Información Geográfica (Universidad Nacional de General Sarminent) on the basis of author's data.

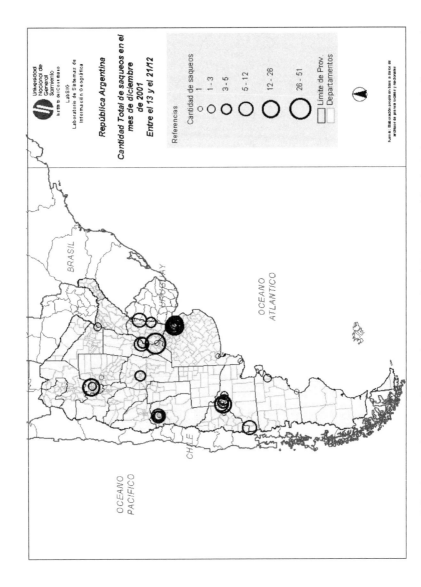

Map 3. The Geographic Distribution of Lootings, Total. Map created by the Laboratorio de Sistemas de Información Geográfica (Universidad Nacional de General Sarminent) on the basis of author's data.

veritable landscape of violent protest (Auyero 2002). Sieges of (and attacks on) public buildings (government houses, legislatures, court-houses), barricades on national and provincial roads, and sit-ins in central plazas became widespread in the south (the provinces of Neuquén, Rio Negro, Santa Cruz, and Tierra del Fuego), center (Córdoba and Santa Fe), and north (Jujuy, Salta, Santiago del Estero, Corrientes, and Chaco, among others) of the country.[1]

The events of December 2001 – the wave of food riots occurred along-side thousands of people blockading roads and bridges throughout the country and banging pots and pans in the main plaza of Buenos Aires in a collective mobilization that, together with heightened elite factionalism, provoked the ousting of two presidents in less than a month[2] – indicate that this historical shift in claims making is still under way. Despite their simultaneous occurrence, road-blocking (*cortes de ruta*), rallies in plazas (*marchas*), and lootings (*saqueos*) are dissimilar forms of collec-tive action with different actors, organizations, collective identities, and dynamics.

The peak of collective action during 2001 has been the subject of many scholarly (Cafassi 2002; Fradkin 2002; Lewkowics 2002), jour-nalistic (Bonasso 2002; Martinez 2002; Camarasa 2002), and insiders' accounts (Kohan 2002; Colectivo Situaciones 2002). Central as they were in generating a terminal political crisis, the lootings, however, remain an uncharted terrain for social scientists. The few existing studies and journalistic reports on the food riots in particular are single-actor accounts dominated by what sociologist Charles Tilly (2003) calls the "steam boiler" analogy or what historian E. P. Thompson (1994) labels a "spasmodic view" of popular revolt. In other words, the main actors in the lootings are said to be the poor and unemployed who, responding to a

---

[1] For different examinations of the causes and forms of the emerging repertoire of col-lective contention, see Villalón 2002; Giarraca 2001; Dinerstein 2001; Scribano and Schuster 2001; Oviedo 2001; Iñigo Carrera 1999; Laufer and Spiguel 1999; Svampa and Pereyra 2003.

[2] President De la Rua governed from May 1999 until December 2001 when he resigned in the midst of the unprecedented politicoeconomic crisis and mass protests. A quick succession of three different presidents (all belonging to the Peronist Party) ended when Duhalde, a former governor of Buenos Aires, was elected by the Parliament to become interim president.

rapid reduction in the standard of living by visible government (in)action (e.g., the suspension of many food distribution programs) and the high level of joblessness (in December unemployment rates were 21 percent of the economically active population), suddenly exploded in anger and plundered stores and supermarkets (Fradkin 2002). As prevailing analysts in Argentina portray the events, poverty and unemployment, together with state inaction, created an insurmountable pressure that built up during 2001 until everything exploded. Most tellingly, the title of a widely publicized book on the 2001 events is *Olla a Presión*, or "pressure cooker" (Cafassi 2002).

Lootings varied in terms of their location, number of participants, type of store attacked, and the presence of police and party brokers among the crowds. As the maps clearly show, lootings were unevenly distributed in broad geographic terms. One-third of the 289 episodes reported in newspapers (a combination of lootings and attempted lootings repressed by the police and/or store owners) occurred in Buenos Aires (96), the most populated province, mainly in the area known as the Conurbano (the metropolitan area surrounding the federal capital). Another 20 percent occurred in Santa Fe (61), the third-most-populated province. Around 10 percent each occurred in the two southern states of Neuquén (29) and Rio Negro (27) and the northern state of Tucumán (27), and the remaining 49 episodes were scattered over seven other provinces. Eleven provinces had no reported episodes during the week.

Number of actors involved also varied. The number of participants ranged from thousands in episodes occurring in Concordia (Entre Ríos), Banda del Rio Salí (Tucumán), and Centenario (Neuquén), to dozens in many smaller episodes in Rosario (Santa Fe), Guaymallén (Mendoza), and Paraná (Entre Ríos). Of the episodes with participant-count information, the modal category of estimated participants was between 100 and 400 (close to 70 percent).

Locally, the crowds attacked different types of targets as well. Nearly 60 percent of the episodes reported by newspapers took place in small, local markets and grocery stores, close to a third occurred in big, chain-owned supermarkets, and 8 percent occurred at nonfood sites (shoe stores, clothing stores, appliance stores, etc.). Police presence was reported in 106 of the 289 episodes (37 percent), sometimes outnumbered by the looters, other times not, sometimes deterring the crowds with rubber bullets and tear gas (and in a few reported cases with real bullets), other times dissuading potential looters simply by their presence (more details on the police presence and actions later). The number of arrests also varied widely from province to province, from dozens in Entre Ríos, to approximately 200 in Rosario, to close to 600 in Tucumán.[3] Successful lootings and those effectively stopped by restraint were evenly distributed when the targets were big, chain-owned supermarkets. When incidents occurred in small, local markets and grocery stores, successful lootings outnumbered rebuffed attempts by nearly three to one. Based on a statistical analysis of newspaper reports, it can be asserted that the odds of police presence at a looting site are 268 percent higher when the site is a large chain supermarket (see Appendix).

The fact that police response was uneven across market types concurs with reports that the state police and the National Guard took special care when it came to protecting stores like the French-owned Carrefour or the American-owned Norte, while at the same time creating the "liberated zone" about which grassroots activists and, as we will later see, shopkeepers spoke. "The police acted very well," said an owner of one of the largest supermarket chains in Rosario. "Police action was impeccable." Divergent evaluations were offered by, among others, Juan Milito, the head of Rosario's Shopkeepers Union (*Union de Almaceneros* or "Small Stores") who said: "As always, the small stores were the most damaged . . . the big chains were protected" (*El Ciudadano* December 24, 2001). And in Neuquén, a city far from Rosario, Ramón Fernandez, the *Secretario Gremial del Centro de Empleados de Comercio* also confirmed that "[t]he police concentrated their efforts on *hipermercados*" (*Rio Negro* December 23, 2001).[4] Further evidence comes from newspaper reports around the country: An article from the newspaper

---

[3] Interestingly, in the provinces in which data are available, the overwhelming majority of those arrested had no penal records – confirming what classic studies on rioting (Caplan 1970; Caplan and Paige 1968; Moinat et al. 1972) assert: Looters are not the tiny criminal minority in poverty enclaves.

[4] The main Argentine newspaper reported that the French-owned supermarkets Auchan and Carrefour were protected by the state police and the National Guard because the French ambassador, Paul Dijoud, called the then–secretary to the president, Nicolás Gallo, asking him to do so (*Clarín*, May 19, 2002).

El Ciudadano (published in Rosario, Santa Fe) spoke of the "relative advantage of the *hipermercados*" during the looting (December 21): "*El Libertad* had a patrol group of the Gendarmería with a truck parked in its parking lot... *Carrefour* and *Micropack* had pre-assigned guards." The newspaper *Página12*, edited in Buenos Aires, asserted that, according to police information, the smallest markets (local grocery stores prominent among them) were the ones that suffered the most looting. Most of the deaths occurred in those episodes when looters or bystanders were killed by store owners attempting to guard their property.

In Buenos Aires, the state police incurred most of their injuries, and they used most of their 73,000 rubber bullets and 2,800 tear gas bombs, in confrontations occurring in front of the *hipermercados* (*Clarín*, May 19, 2002). A case in point is the brutal police repression of a looting that took place in front of a *Carrefour* supermarket, while dozens of small, unguarded stores were being sacked nearby and all over Buenos Aires. A highly perceptive observer of police behavior (and former undersecretary of security in the state of Buenos Aires) speaks of "evident police passivity" during the lootings and adds that it is quite common for the *bonaerense* to "liberate" or free certain zones so that criminal activity can proceed without police presence (Sain 2004).[5] As the lootings were taking place, journalists' reports from several media noted that the Buenos Aires police were "not very disposed to intervene" (Kollmann, December 20, 2001), and the National Guard (*Gendarmería*), the Federal Police, and the Naval Police (*Prefectura*) had a similar diagnosis.

Interpretations regarding police inaction vary widely: As we will see later, most store owners (those who were looted and those who were spared from violence) and residents (looters or bystanders) think that this was intentional and that it proves the "political" character of the lootings. Many journalists (mainly from *Clarín* and *Página12*) and some grassroots leaders (D'Elia from the *Federación de Tierra y Vivienda* and Alderete from the *Corriente Clasista y Combativa*) believe that police absence was part of a plot (some even used the term "conspiracy") to create the political and

---

[5] This practice of "liberating zones" is also common among Rio de Janeiro's police when dealing with drug trafficking. Arias (2004:3) writes: "Corrupt police fail to enforce the law; they inform traffickers of police activities and set up police operations in places where they will not interfere with trafficking."

social instability that ended De La Rua's government. Interpretations aside, one thing is clear: Police action was indeed uneven, and it did gravitate toward the biggest markets. In an attempt to understand why this was so, I made my way to the offices of Juan José Alvarez, who was the secretary of security for Buenos Aires (i.e., the civilian official in charge of the state police) when the lootings took place. What follows is an accurate-as-possible rendition of the conversation we had in Alvarez's elegant offices in the exclusive barrio of La Recoleta regarding police activity during December 18–20 in the Conurbano Bonaerense.

Enter the Super-Cop

A sharp man in his early fifties, Alvarez seems to be a man on a mission. He is now a member of the House of Representatives and the chief of staff of Hilda Duhalde's electoral campaign, and he is understandably busy. In the past four years, he has been the head of the Bonaerense (during Governor Ruckauf's term) and the head of the Federal Police (during Duhalde's presidency). Few men around know the inner workings of the police forces better than he does.

He greets me, offers coffee, and opens our chat with what looks like a compliment: "Which book of yours have I read?" I told him he probably remembers my *Poor People's Politics* (a study of the clientelist practices of his own Peronist Party) and, without answering, he asks: "What do you want to know?" I replied with a simple: "All you remember about the *saqueos* from 2001." "I will tell you the very truth of what happened," he says. The first important thing to remember, he emphasizes, is that the lootings "did not start in Buenos Aires but in the provinces.... Of course, when something occurs in the Conurbano it has a different relevance. I had just taken office as the secretary of security, and the lootings began on the eighteenth in some scattered places in Buenos Aires. In San Miguel, [the mayor] Rico, who had been the head of the Bonaerense before me and had good contacts inside the force, talked to the police chief and got more police forces in his district ... that's why nothing happened in San Miguel.... On the nineteenth, I woke up and I got a call from a radio program asking me if I was going to start police action [*la represión*] and I said, 'No.'"

According to police reports he received early that day, the crowds were not easily dispersed – they were, he said, "like soccer gangs, with some level of internal organization." He then decided to "prevent further looting using only antimutiny police." The state police had few "antimutiny elements," he states, "but I decided to use only those. I gave explicit orders: Those who lacked antimutiny equipment should leave the scene, should go home and stay with their families. My orders were clear: The police should move out, should kill nobody. That's when I said: 'I would rather lament the loss of a can of tomatoes than the loss of a life.'" (This statement was broadcasted on radio and is published in the December 20 edition of *Clarín*.) "In order to control the lootings," he tells me, "you need numbers and equipment." The Bonaerense had neither, he says, and, "I had to protect the most important points [*los puntos neurálgicos*]. . . . There are TV images that show a cop moving out from the looting scene, as if not willing to do anything. They criticized me a lot for that. And, truth be told, that cop left because he didn't have antimutiny elements. What do you want him to do? To shoot? *There were no 'liberated zones', there were areas that were insufficiently protected. There's an important difference between the two*" [my emphasis].

I couldn't quite tell the difference, and he noticed my puzzled face. I told him about the dataset that I had compiled based on newspaper accounts that clearly shows police forces gravitating toward big chain supermarkets independently of the number of looters on the scene [see Appendix]. At that point, the best moment in a very interesting two-hour-long interview took place – one of those moments interviewers and/or ethnographers hope for. He stood up, opened the door and called Cacho, one of his private secretaries, in. Without telling Cacho what we were talking about, he asked him:

ALVAREZ: Cacho, what did Coto [Alfredo Coto is the owner of a large chain of supermarkets] want during the 2001 lootings?

CACHO: Horses [a reference to the mounted police] . . .

ALVAREZ: What did we send him?

CACHO: Nothing . . .

ALVAREZ: Come on, Cacho, you can tell him. How many horses did Coto want?

CACHO: Seventy . . .

ALVAREZ: And, how many did we send him?

CACHO: Four.

ALVAREZ (looking straight at me): See. Now, if you have four horses, where do you send them? To Coto or to the grocery store Los Purretes in Hurlingham [the name of a small store in his district]?

Food Lootings

JAVIER: To Coto?

ALVAREZ: There's your dataset!

The police, he agrees, protected the big markets more than the small ones, because "there was more commotion there.... Coto and Los Purretes are different things.... I told the police to pull out, I told them to go home and rest, I told them that those who lack antimutiny equipment should stay out. With the police of Buenos Aires, you have to give clear orders. It is either North or South. If you tell them, Northwest, the guys will do a disaster. You can't tell them to act only when they are threatened, because you will leave a lot of room for their discretion and that's very dangerous.... Nobody was killed during the lootings."

Alvarez had many other things to say about the participation (or lack thereof) of the Peronist Party as the motor behind the lootings and about the meanings of the episodes (see Chapter 4). What concerns me in this section is his rationale behind the police's selective inattention during the lootings. He summarized it for me in the following way: "It is true. The police moved away. The Conurbano does not have enough police forces. There's no antimutiny police. If I have four horses, where do I send them, to Coto or to Los Purretes?"

Lootings did not unfold, to quote geographer Doreen Massey, "on the head of a pin, in a spaceless, geographically undifferentiated world" (1984:4). The geography of policing came to reinforce an already existing built environment during the protection of foreign-owned chain supermarkets. Characteristically, Auchans, Carrefours, Discos, and Jumbos are surrounded by highways, railways, and/or large avenues, accessible mostly by car or public transportation. Copresence, the essential ingredient in the making of a looting [and of any other kind of contentious collective action (e.g., McAdam 1982; Sewell 2002; Tilly 2003; Auyero 2006)], is thus constrained by sheer physical location.[6] Most *hipermercados* are also fenced off by huge walls and/or are surrounded by parking lots and/or empty spaces. Compared to the typical small store (guarded

---

[6] Note that I said constrained and not altogether prevented because claims for food that could have escalated into lootings took place in these segregated spaces. Typically, these episodes occurred at the beginning of the looting week and were organized by picketers (see next section). Lootings did occur in big chain supermarkets but were the exception.

solely by a roll-up metal blind and easily accessible from the sidewalk) the *hipermercado* is thus easier to be defended by the police and more difficult to be attacked by looters.[7]

This said, it should be added that spatiality is not destiny. Political decisions, more than spatial matters, dictated the fate of small stores.[8] Alfredo Coto and other owners of large supermarkets had a direct line to state officials (as attested by the conversation between Alvarez, Cacho, and myself); the owners of Los Purretes and similar stores did not. Political connections mattered in avoiding violence (we will see in Chapter 4 that this is true even *within* looted areas) but so did routine, power-laden ways of distributing state protection. I have few doubts about the statement regarding the lack of horses – the lack of antimutiny elements in the police forces is well known. I have even fewer doubts about the taken-for-granted character of Alvarez's assertion regarding where those horses should be allocated in case of trouble: Who in his right mind would send the four horses to Los Purretes? The problem with that "obvious" assertion (even I fell victim to it in my reply to Alvarez) is that stores like Los Purretes are usually adjacent to other dozens of small stores – in both Matanza and Moreno, the lootings were concentrated in areas populated by small stores. Early during the looting week, the police of the province of Buenos Aires decided to take special care of the *hipermercados*, while not making any sort of special provision for other commercial areas that were likely to be the object of looting activity (because looting had occurred in the past, i.e., in 1989 and 1990, and because rumors in the area, rumors that the police could have hardly ignored, were rampant days before the lootings actually began). The two sites of

---

[7] For the central role played by spatial considerations in the ways in which the police think and feel about their actions, see Hathazy (2004).

[8] In his insightful study of the Infantry Guard (*Guardia de Infantería*) of Córdoba's state police, Paul Hathazy (2004:12) shows that the "decision or disposition" to supress street mobilizations by this specialized branch of the police "is determined by a political decision, by what they (the police agents) call 'the political climate' or by the '*líneas que se bajan políticamente.*'" Force members are, according to his analysis, very aware of the crucial influence of political decisions on the way in which they deal with political conflict: if there is a (political) command that forbids repression, then they do not act, they "endure" –"*se aguanta,*" as members of the guard put it. One police agent told Hathazy: "If we do not acknowledge the fact that political influence is a constant in the Infantry Guard's work, we cannot keep talking."

heaviest looting in Greater Buenos Aires (Crovara and Cristianía in Matanza and El Cruce de Castelar in Moreno) could have been protected by the police in the same way they protected the *hipermercados* (by cordoning off the area, a task that would have been easy given the size of the streets and the extension of the commercial area). The fact is that the police did not do so, and that explains, to a great extent, the devastation that occurred in both areas.[9] The question I should have posed to Alvarez then is the following: If you have four horses, would you send them to a single big Coto or to El Cruce the Castelar, the site of at least fifty small stores? Somehow, I know his answer.[10]

Detailed newspaper reports exist for fewer than half of the recorded 289 episodes. Newspapers and investigative journalists' accounts provide some sort of detailed descriptions of the composition and actions of the looting crowds in approximately 130 episodes. In half of these reports, reporters noted the presence of Peronist Party brokers among the crowds, particularly at the two sites of the heaviest looting activity – La Matanza and Moreno – and particularly in the lootings that occurred in small stores with little police presence. In small-store lootings, in addition to the lower likelihood of police presence, there is a higher visibility of party brokers (see Appendix). Investigative journalists' reports and

---

[9] The response of state government forces is a crucial factor in determining the onset and development of collective violence. Wilkinson (2004:86) provides one clear example: "In 1992, when Hindu-Muslim riots broke out throughout India after the destruction of the Ayodhya mosque, Bihar was one of the few states to remain peaceful. [Chief Minister] Laloo Yadav, when asked to explain why Bihar had been so quiet despite its woeful record of past riots, explained how his government had arrested returning militants from Uttar Pradesh (the site of Ayodhya) before they could reach their towns and villages, and how he had threatened all districts' magistrates and police station officers with the loss of their jobs if they allowed any riots to break out in their towns. 'The political will of the state government' he said, 'was clear.'" In Buenos Aires, this political will was also clear, but bifurcated (strong protection to chain markets; no protection to small ones).

[10] Truth be told, police "underprotection" of small markets, though striking during the lootings, is part of everyday life in poor areas. Most of the store owners we interviewed in La Matanza, for example, told us that they have been robbed during the last year (2004–5), and that the police didn't do much about it. As Pablo, whose sneaker store in Crovara y Cristianía was looted in December 2001, told us, "We all know who the thieves are here, and the police never do anything about them. The police are around, they are here. We go and talk to them. But today there's one chief, tomorrow there's another one . . . and everything keeps being the same."

our own interviews point to some sort of connection between the presence of party brokers and the virtual absence (or inaction) of police in small-store looting. This connection (a) draws attention to the existence of the gray zone of politics and (b) highlights the continuities between routine politics and collective violence. The next chapter will explore this connection in as detailed a form as the available evidence allows. But, before attempting that, let me further parse and contextualize the lootings.

Picketers, Not Looters

The heavy looting activity that occurred between December 18 and 21 in the Conurbano was preceded by lootings in the provinces and by collective claims for food that were made by organizations of unemployed workers (known as *piqueteros*) in front of chain supermarkets (*hipermercados*). It is interesting to detail what happened in these episodes because they illustrate, as sorts of counterfactuals, what might (or might not) have happened during a looting. In a nutshell, these events tell us what occurred when massive claims for food were *visibly* coordinated by one or more organizations that (a) were able to mobilize their supporters to focus on large supermarkets (the unemployed organizations' political orientations guided their choice of target) and (b) were able to control, to a certain extent, their supporters, so that the minor contingencies that proved key in the lootings in small markets did not take place (someone throwing a stone and breaking a window or another one attempting to shatter a roller blind). These episodes illustrate *coordination* in claims making, which are different in form and dynamic from the looting episodes that had the *creation of opportunities* by party brokers and police agents as their main feature. In the first case, the leaders of the *piqueteros* brought their members to big chain supermarkets and negotiated on their behalf with supermarkets' managers and authorities (police chiefs) regarding the distribution of food. In the second case, as we'll see in greater detail later, brokers spread rumors about the distribution of food at a small market and/or matter-of-factly informed people that looting was going to occur (and no repression would ensue) while police agents (a) were absent, (b) were present but inactive, and/or (c) were

88

present and collaborated in the looting. These early organized claims for food at large supermarkets also anticipated the care that repressive forces would take in the protection of chain stores.

The December 15 cover of the popular newspaper *Crónica* states that "Carrefour is besieged by the poor: They are demanding food." More than a hundred of "the unemployed and needy... carrying sticks and mobilized by the *Corriente Clasista y Combativa*" surround Carrefour and ask for food. Antimutiny police forces are deployed to "avoid the sacking." Things get tense, the newspaper informs us, when a group of *manifestantes* armed with sticks, iron bars, and slings, move close to the store's entrance. In a scene that will hardly be seen in small stores, "police authorities act cautiously to avoid incidents." In a display of force that, again, is almost unthinkable in places like El Cruce in Moreno or the crossroads of Crovara and Cristianía in Matanza with their high concentration of small grocery stores, butcher shops, clothing stores, and the like, the local police forces are "aided by members of the *Bonaerense* [provincial police force]." The supermarket is "cordoned off" by the police, and soon a massive distribution of food is organized at the site.

Two days later, and still before the colossal lootings of December 18–21, the same newspaper reports that in the south of the Conurbano Bonaerense, hundreds of unemployed persons block the roads in front of three chain supermarkets (Carrefour, Auchan, and Jumbo) demanding bags of food and unemployment subsidies (note that, different from the lootings that explode days later, these collective actions have specific demands). The newspaper, citing police informants, asserts that the state police are boosting the security measures at twenty supermarkets in the area: "Given the possibility of lootings, there are more police rounds and more protection in the area stores. We decided to increase police rounds in the stores of chain supermarkets in Adrogué, Transradio, Lomas de Zamora, Temperley, Marmol and Lanús." Police informants also point out that (a) supermarket chains might decide to voluntarily distribute bags of food in order to calm down the situation (something that actually happened later and that, together with police protection and sheer geographical inaccessibility, prevented looting of big supermarkets), and (b) they do not rule out rising "social tension" during the next weekend (an assertion that soon proves to be an understatement given the massiveness of looting activity throughout the Conurbano).

Looting in Hipermercados

In December 2001, Liliana Vargas, Angela Cáceres, and Roxana Frias were living in the city of Tucumán. They and their husbands were unemployed and, according to them, had "several kids to feed." Together with another 150 women, they walked to a municipal center where, "We were told the government was giving out food." When they showed up, however, nobody was there to help them. They then went to a chain supermarket, Gomez Pardo, where they understood food was being distributed. As soon as they arrived, police fired rubber bullets and tear gas at the crowd. "The government lied to us," they said afterward. "We came to ask for food, and they held us back as if we were criminals."

The women's story contains key elements that were present in most of the lootings that took place in big chain supermarkets. Poor people initially gathered in front of these supermarkets because rumors [a form of communication that is usually quite central in riots (Rosnow 1988; Kakar 1996)] concerning the prompt distribution of food were running rampant through the neighborhood. Groups of people, in most cases composed mostly of women and children, would arrive and silently and peaceably assemble at their doors. Once the group had gathered, one of three scenarios was likely. In one scenario, they were summarily repelled with rubber and/or real bullets and tear gas by the police or National Guard, as was the case with Liliana and her friends. In these episodes, no actual looting was allowed to take place. This repression sometimes took place while lootings were taking place in small markets located nearby.

In another likely scenario, the police or National Guard was present, but they did not fire their guns, and negotiations ensued. The store manager or owner promised the delivery of food boxes to avert the looting, and members of the crowds negotiated the exact number of boxes. If the negotiations were successful, the crowd would dissolve, and, again, no looting ensued. In many cases, these negotiations were supervised by the police. Negotiations sometimes involved public authorities who, especially toward the beginning and the end of the week of looting (mainly on December 14 and December 21), showed up with food boxes from state-supported programs to prevent the looting as in the case of the supermarket Azul (one of the largest chains in Rosario). In this particular instance, the secretary of welfare turned up in the middle of the police (who were engaged in repressive actions) and promised the immediate distribution of food products. "Things soon calmed down," a reporter from *El Ciudadano* wrote on December 15. Other times, negotiations involved police chiefs such as in front of the Carrefour branch in Moreno. Following is journalist Laura Vales' description of what happened there (*Página12 Digital*, December 20, 2001):

> There's confusion in front of the gates [of Carrefour], nobody knows exactly what to do. Some push forward to enter [the premises], others ask [adults] to take children to the back. Nobody can tell whether the police will fire their guns or not. The chief of police [*Comisario Inspector*] Cabrera stands up on a supermarket cart and asks for silence.
>
> "This situation has blown up [*eclosionó*]," the chief screams in front of 800 neighbors. "Even if they give you a bag a food, you'll face the same problem five days from now. The same thing is going on throughout the province, and we have to dialogue among ourselves, so that we don't set the fire right here in Moreno. I do not want to fight [*combatir*] against you. I repeat: I do not want to fight against you."
>
> The chief orders the only cameraman to shut his camera off and continues:
>
> "I was also duped, they also stole from me [*A mi también me metieron la mano en el bolsillo*]."
>
> People applaud him. Encouraged, the chief tells the people to go to the municipality, and people boo him.
>
> "We want food, not promises," a thin guy answers him [. . .]
>
> "Go to the Plaza de Mayo, with the mayor" [see Chapter 4].
>
> But the people are now screaming louder: "We want to eat." "What do they think?" a woman asks, "Do they think I'm going to walk all the way to Plaza de Mayo for a packet of sugar?"

In a third possible scenario, negotiations were not altogether successful even when the police were present. The case of a looting in Chubut illustrates the "broken-negotiation" dimension of the looting episodes (Tilly 2003). In this episode, the crowd's delegates accepted the promise of distribution of merchandise by the manager of the largest supermarket in the city (Comodoro Rivadavia), but when the content of the boxes was found wanting, the crowds – vastly outnumbering the police – broke into the premises and took away merchandise. Negotiations also went awry from more minor contingencies. A youngster would throw a rock at the window of a supermarket, for example, or a small group within a much larger crowd would not accept any sort of deal, triggering mayhem. The typical looting scene in big supermarkets included what many newspapers called a "looting vanguard," composed mostly of youngsters and minors who, being used to police harassment, took advantage of this unique opportunity (having the police outnumbered) to carry out a face-to-face confrontation with the forces of order. Here's how a reporter described a confrontation between the "looting vanguard" (also present in lootings in small markets) and the police. This particular episode occurred in the city of Neuquén, in the southwestern province of the same name.

> "Come on, come on, come on . . . we'll move them [the cops] out [*vamos que los rajamos*]." These are the voices of young kids who are insulting the police, who are attacking the cops with rocks and their own bodies. The kids . . . know the logic very well . . . they never cease to be on the offensive: sooner or later the police will be out of rubber bullets and tear gas canisters. And, it is well known, there are always rocks. When the battle is more intense on one side, the youngsters reappear on another side to disorient the police. With this strategy . . . hundreds of looters are wearing the police down. I am at the corner of Belgrano and Combate de San Lorenzo, a few yards from a Topsy supermarket. [. . .] Some neighbors witness the curious spectacle . . . A 16-year-old kid . . . is caught by the police. Four or five cops clean the floor with the kid's body . . . two or three cops kick and punch the kid, who is exhausted. The public insults the police, *yuta* or *cana hija de puta*. . . . It is almost 3 A.M. and the police secure the corner. The rocks can now be seen lying on the asphalt, burning tires illuminate the streets. The night seems to have devoured the invisible gang of stone-throwing kids. The police have five kids lying down, "kissing" the asphalt with their hands on their backs. (*Rio Negro*, December 21, 2001)[11]

[11] For an insightful account of the deep-seated (and widely justified) contempt that shantytown youngsters have for the police, see Alarcón (2003).

Figure 6. Protecting Small Markets.

Small Markets Get Sacked

In December 2001, Josefa was living in a small shack located in a poor neighborhood of Moreno. On the eighteenth, she received a small flyer inviting her to "bust" a group of markets. The next day, she showed up on time in front of Kin, and soon 200 people were gathered in front of this small market clamoring for food. She recalls seeing a police car leaving the scene and a man who worked at the local municipality talking on his cellular phone. Soon, a truck loaded with a *grupo de pesados* (or group of thugs), known in the neighborhood as "*Los Gurkas*," arrived at the scene. "They broke the doors and called us in," Josefa remembers. "A few days later, I met one of them, and he told me that people from the Peronist Party paid 100 pesos for the job." Far from Josefa, in another poor enclave in Buenos Aires, residents of the barrio Baires (located in the municipality of Tigre) seemed to have received similar news about an imminent looting through their children: "When my son arrived home from school, he told me that a man from the local *Unidad Básica* (Peronist Party's grassroots office) came to inform the teachers about the sites of the lootings. The teacher told my son that she was going to go. And we went to see if we could get something" (*Clarín*, May 19, 2002).

In the lootings that took place in small markets, public authorities were almost never present, and store owners were less prepared to negotiate with the crowd to more peacefully distribute food. However, once the groups had gathered in front of neighborhood supermarkets or grocery stores, owners occasionally distributed food and averted looting; in others, owners barricaded themselves in their stores and shot at the crowds (as shown in Figure 6). These occasions proved to be fatal for looters: At least a dozen were killed, and many more were injured by store owners. In most cases, however, nothing other than police repression (which tended to be absent in the majority of these cases), prevented the crowds from breaking into these stores and seizing whatever they could (rumors about impending, but seldom materialized, police actions usually ran rampant at the site, so looting always proceeded at a fast pace). In most episodes when police arrived at all, it was after the premises were completely sacked.

What seems to be common to most of these episodes is that "the crowd" was, in fact, composed of small *groups* that would arrive *together* at the looting site giving plausibility to the theoretical arguments made about the existing linkages among participants in joint action, destructive or otherwise. As Aveni (1977) would say, looters were a "not-so-lonely crowd" (see also McPhail and Wohlstein 1983).[12] Recent research on contentious politics (McAdam, Tarrow, and Tilly 2001; Diani and McAdam 2003) and on collective violence (Tilly 2003) highlights precisely this aspect of collective action episodes: "In practice," writes Tilly (2003:32), "constituents' units of claim-making actors often consist not of living, breathing whole individuals but of groups, organizations, bundles of social relations, and social sites such as occupations and neighborhoods." Most scholarship on collective action highlights the existence of *horizontal ties* between protesting parties – so much so that formal or informal relations among individuals work as a sort of precondition for their joining in social movement activity (see, for example, McAdam

---

[12] As highlighted in the Introduction, this was also the case in post-Katrina lootings, as well as in the November riots in France.

1988).[13] *Vertical connections* between insurgents and authorities, however, have deserved much less attention. Some of the looting crowds were also "connected" in this second sense of the term as evidenced by the presence of party brokers among looters, sometimes reported to be directing the crowds to and from their targets (Young 2002). In order to figure out exactly how these two types of connection (between looters themselves and between looters, cops, and brokers) matter in the making of the looting, we need to look more microscopically at specific incidents. That is the task of the next chapter.

[13] Analysts of the recent wave of riots in France (November 2005), also highlight the importance of these ties among young participants. See, among others, Roy (2006) and Silverstein and Tetreault (2006).

4

Moreno and La Matanza Lootings

> [T]here is no contradiction between the fact that, on the one hand, mob violence may be highly organized and crowds provided with such instruments as voter's lists or combustible powders, and on the other that crowds draw upon repositories of unconscious images.... Hence, just as we study the organization and networks through which crowds are recruited, so must we document the organizing images, including rumours, that crowds use to define themselves and their victims.
>
> Veena Das

Thus far, most of the reconstruction has been based on secondary sources (newspaper accounts, police reports, video footage, investigative journalists' descriptions). I now turn to my own fieldwork, which took place in Moreno and La Matanza. In Moreno, the following evidence comes mostly from El Cruce de Castelar (site of dozens of small stores, many of them looted during the week under investigation, hereafter El Cruce) and from Lomas Verde, a poor barrio located fifteen blocks from El Cruce from which many of the looters came. In the case of La Matanza, the evidence comes from the crossroads of Crovara and Cristianía (site of heavy looting activity, hereafter C&C) and from BID, a poor enclave situated thirteen blocks from it (also known as Barrio Villegas). In what follows I draw on in-depth interviews with owners, managers, and employees of stores located in both sites, with brokers of the Peronist Party and grassroots activists, and with residents of both barrios who either themselves participated in the lootings or knew someone who did.

Moreno is a district located in the western part of the Conurbano Bonaerense, thirty-seven kilometers from the federal capital. It has one of the lowest values on the Human Development Index[1] (the second-lowest in Buenos Aires, following only the district of Florencio Varela) (Alsina and Catenazzi 2002) as close to a third of its 380,000 inhabitants have "unsatisfied basic needs." La Matanza is a district that borders the federal capital on the southwest; it ranks eighth on the Human Development Index (Alsina and Catenazzi 2002) with half of its 1,255,288 inhabitants living under the poverty line (for a description, see Cerrutti and Grimson 2004). La Matanza is the most populated district in the Conurbano, with 106 shantytowns (Torresi 2005). Both La Matanza and Moreno share the plight that has affected the whole region since the early 1990s: skyrocketing poverty due to hyperunemployment. In May 1997, 24.8 percent of households in the Conurbano (and 32.7 percent of the population) were living below the poverty line. By May 2003, these figures had almost doubled: 50.5 percent of the households (and 61.3 percent of the population) were in that condition (Indec 2003).

Field Notes, July 17, 2004
Delia lives with her brother and her three kids in Lomas Verde. She's been involved in politics for twenty years, always as a member of the Peronist Party. She is now a *manzanera* – a block coordinator for the *Plan Vida* – and heads a small cooperative that is building housing units with funds provided by the local state. She is a Peronist broker, mediating between the mayor and his clients – she distributes resources that she obtains through her connections in the municipal building ("I have a phone number I can call in case I need something") and channels support from below, handing out ballots during election times ("among my people") – and organizing the now (in)famous pre- and postelection barbecues.

Asked about the December lootings, she smiles and replies: "What do you want to know? What did we take?" Sensing that she is sort of defending herself, I react with, "No, no... I'd like to know how was it? How did you find out?" Her response encapsulates one crucial dynamic of the looting: "We [the members of the party] knew about the lootings

---

[1] The Human Development Index (*Indice de Desarrollo Humano*) as defined by the UNDP comprises three elements: health (life expectancy), education (combined index of literacy and school attendance), and living conditions (estimated through per capita income utility) (Alsina and Catenazzi 2002).

beforehand. Around 1 A.M. [the lootings began by noon] we knew that there was going to be a looting [*sabíamos que se iba a saquear*]. We were told about them, and we passed the information along [among the members of the party]." She recounts that she went back and forth along the fifteen-block stretch between her home and El Cruce [the area in which most stores were located] six times. I then ask her about police presence in the area.

JAVIER: Weren't you afraid of the cops?

DELIA: Not at all; they were worse than us. They were the ones who took most of the things . . . and, when we were inside [the supermarket] El Chivo, they even told us where to escape so that we wouldn't get in trouble.

A recollection of the "stuff she got" leads her into a reflection of the aftermath of the lootings: "I took cleaning products, cream, shampoo, hair dye. . . . Right after the lootings, the neighbors began to exchange things. Those who had noodles exchanged them for meat. I didn't buy any meat for three months. With the hair dye, I charged five pesos per dye."

She then concludes: "For once, the people had the chance to eat a piece of [gourmet] cheese, a kind of cheese that they'd never tried before. It was the best Christmas we had. We were all happy. We ate a lot, we drank champagne and the best wines." And her brother adds: "You saw smoke coming from everywhere, everybody was barbecuing. Everybody had new clothes and toys for their children."

The end of 2001 found the inhabitants of Moreno and La Matanza, as those of many other poor areas throughout the country, struggling to make ends meet with record-high levels of unemployment and shrinking state assistance. Food-assistance and other welfare programs (most notably, unemployment subsidies) had been steadily declining since the Congress passed Law 25,453 publicly known as "*Déficit Cero*" (Zero Deficit Law) in July 2001: "In October, 2001, soon after the implementation of the Zero Deficit Law, the budgets of the food programs belonging to the Ministry of Social Welfare (whose beneficiaries amount to 2.5 million persons) were not appropriated" (CELS 2002). As the then–minister of labor of Buenos Aires (now minister of the interior at the national level) told me, "The federal government was cutting, cutting, cutting [social programs]."

Karina, a resident of one of the most destitute enclaves in Moreno, remembers that at the time she had an unemployment subsidy (then known as *Plan Trabajar*), but the monthly payments were delayed (something that was quite common throughout the district and throughout the Conurbano): "They were supposed to be paying by the end of the month [November] and they didn't. They would set a date, then another one. Christmas was right around the corner and . . . well, then the lootings happened." Payments for the unemployment subsidies were not only delayed but dwindling. After describing the long lines of unemployed people who had been waiting to receive their checks since very early in the morning, a reporter from a Moreno newspaper (*Para Ud!* 2001:8) wrote: "a crowd of beneficiaries from the *Plan Trabajar* were waiting at the Banco Provincia to receive their 160 *patacones* [government bonds]. . . . Since July, government charity went down from 200 *pesos* to 160 *patacones*. When the welfare program began, beneficiaries used to receive their checks every other week; since then benefits began to be delayed for 30 to 35 days."

Lootings in El Cruce began late on December 18, but the heaviest amount of looting activity (in which the most people participated and the most stores were looted) took place on the afternoon of December 19. That day witnessed most of the destruction in La Matanza, too. Days before, neighbors, looters, and shopkeepers knew "something was coming." Sandra, who stayed home in Lomas Verde during the episodes, told us that a week or so in advance she found out through a neighbor that lootings were going to take place. Mono, who did loot, told us: "I was in school, and my classmates and friends were talking about the lootings like two weeks before it all began." "In Moreno," Mónica Gomez told journalist Laura Vales (Vales 2001), "we knew that the lootings were going to happen for at least about a month, but nobody did anything. They gave us [unemployment] subsidies, and then they cut them. They gave us bags of food, but they suddenly stopped giving them. Nobody can take that. *Así nadie aguanta*." Much like in the lootings that took place in *hipermercados*, rumors were also running rampant among shopkeepers in El Cruce and in C&C.

"Sure, there were rumors saying that people were coming from
Moreno to sack, that they were coming from everywhere . . . ."

"There was a lot of gossip saying that the sackings were about to
start."

"A week or so before, other shopkeepers and customers were spreading rumors that there was a group of people who were going to
create *disturbios*."

"That morning I was here in the store, and there were rumors going
around. They said there were going to be lootings. At 10 A.M. the
police told us to close the stores. We went home at noon, but we
were scared something was going to happen."

And, similar to the lootings in big supermarkets, some rumors pointed
to specific actions that were about to take place and that proved to be
central in triggering the incidents. In one specific case, cited by many,
"people were saying" that food was going to be distributed by Disco,
a big chain supermarket close to El Cruce. Another rumor informed
BID residents that lootings had been prevented in nearby Auchan, and
that looters were approaching C&C. Tamara and many other neighbors
agree: "People were saying that Disco was about to give out food. They
didn't give anything, so people headed to El Cruce." Shopkeepers concur: "People began to gather at Disco because there was a rumor that said
they were giving out food there. And it was a lie . . . so they all came to El
Cruce."

No rumor, however, could have prepared shopkeepers for what they
witnessed: Hundreds of children, women, men, "young, for the most
part . . . but old people too," who were "our own customers" broke into
dozens of stores (food stores, but also clothing stores, bazaars, wholesale
stores with no food products in them, small kiosks, etc.) and took the
merchandise away.

The field note I included about Delia does not convey the hesitancy
that people who looted still show when recollecting the episodes. Some
use the third person to refer to their own actions, others say that they
only went there to look, others that they only stayed outside the looted
stores, and others that they took less merchandise than they actually
did. The following exchange illustrates some of this caution (both at the

looting scene and in the recollection). It takes place at María's house in Lomas Verde between her, her brother Carlos, and Carlos's son.

> CARLOS: I was at home and was watching the looting on TV. And people were in the streets coming back from El Cruce. And a friend of mine [Hector] showed up, and we said, "Let's go and see what's going on." I went to see what was happening . . . and maybe to "rescue" something . . .

> MARÍA: I had to push him [Carlos] because he was simply looking, and he wouldn't dare to go inside [the store]. But then he liked it, and he went once, twice, six times total. Until recently I used a broom he brought me . . .

> CARLOS'S SON: Papi, do you remember that you and Hector brought back like forty pairs of pants?

> MARÍA: People would bring anything. Some of the stores that you now see in this barrio began with the lootings. They took freezers, furniture, merchandise, and they opened their own business with that.

The dialogue illustrates two important factors during the onset of the lootings. As some of our interviewees told us, many found out about the lootings through the TV. But most of them realized something was happening when they saw their neighbors rushing by shouting, "*Están saqueando! Están saqueando!* [They are looting]." Almost all of our interviewees recalled seeing someone running through the alleyways or the streets conveying the news. In other words, the spread of information occurred through both interpersonal ties and indirect and impersonal channels. Relational and nonrelational diffusion reinforced each other (Tarrow 2005; McAdam and Rucht 1993). Once information about the occurrence of the lootings became widespread, a more specific mechanism began to operate: mutual signaling. In what follows, we will see how neighbors and friends indicated to each other when and where it was safe to loot. We will later examine what part political brokers played in this.

The looting crowd did not form at the site but was "connected" beforehand. Looters went to the looting scene with trusted others, mostly family members:

> "Yes, I went to El Cruce, but I was scared. . . . I went with my brother. In El Cruce I saw a lot of people I knew, classmates, friends." (Diana)

"First I went with friends, then with my little sister." (Mono)

"I was in El Cruce, and I saw my classmates that were in groups, and they greeted me and smiled at me, and I didn't realize, but they were there because they were about to loot." (Tamara)

"I went with my mum to see what was going on in C&C." (Mario)

"I went after my son Bebe who wanted to loot." (Irma)

Claudia was watching TV that day and at first couldn't believe what she saw; lootings were taking place a couple of blocks from her home in Lomas Verde, where she did most of her shopping on a daily basis: "My aunt and my daughter wanted to go. My daughter wanted to know what a looting was all about. We went to El Cruce, but we didn't bring shopping bags with us. I hadn't gone before because my husband would have gotten very angry at me [*me iba a cagar a pedos*], but then I went anyway. We took this street because there were no cops, and it was calmer there. . . . We got to this supermarket, but . . . I don't know what is to take stuff from inside the store . . . I only took the stuff that other people would throw on the street." Given the goods she came back from El Cruce with, it's hard to believe she was not inside a store. She lists soft drinks, ice cream, olives, sugar, yerba, frankfurters, and noodles. After the listing, she adds: "Before arriving home, I found a bag with school stuff for the kids." Once they realized looting was allowed, looters used the supermarket carts to make several trips to El Cruce. Delia went five to six times, and Pelu many others. Claudia went once, but her sons went several times.

Antonio, another looter, told us: "We went to Caburé [a supermarket located five blocks from his home]. The owner was there, but then the cops advised him to leave. That's when we got in, and we took the stuff. Even the cops put stuff in the police car." A neighbor, who witnessed looting scenes from her house, said, "When they were sacking the butcher shop [across the street], the cops would calm people down and then put all the meat inside their patrol car!" Tamara, who went to El Cruce with two of her sisters, "but just to take a peek" (as many who ended up with stuff from the lootings only dared to admit), describes the crowd as a "herd. They would say: 'Cops coming!' and they would all run and hide. The cops would leave, and they would return, like ants."

"What can I tell you about the police?" asks Claudia, who participated in the lootings, "They were the ones who took most of the stuff, the best things. They would get you and grab your bags. The computer they now have is from the lootings." Noting the differential police protection, a local newspaper (*Para Ud!* 2002:3) describes: "Despite police presence, a hundred or so people began to loot the local stores. Ten hours later, and while a well-known French *hipermercado* located in Gaona and Graham Bell [reference to Carrefour] was heavily guarded [similar kinds of businesses were also protected], shopkeepers and owners of small supermarkets began to suffer the devastation."

These last statements complicate the story I have been telling in the previous chapter based on secondary resources. It is not true, as an account of the lootings solely based on newspaper reports would have it, that the police were *absent* when lootings took place in small markets. The police were present in El Cruce and in C&C: Sometimes police agents collaborated with the ransacking (as the preceding statements depict). At other times they simply witnessed the looting from a distance.[2] Almost every single shopkeeper at both sites mentioned the passive police presence:

> "There were cops... but they had orders not to do anything." (Antonio, El Cruce)
>
> "Cops were patrolling the area with two old patrol cars... they didn't do anything" (Daniel, El Cruce)
>
> MARIO (El Cruce): "There were tons of policemen but there was no order to act as they should [*reprimir como corresponde*].... The chief of police said it publicly; they did not have orders to arrest or do anything...
>
> Q: How did the police react?
>
> MARIO: They didn't act. To be honest, they didn't do anything. Once the store was empty, they threw tear gas.... I guess they did so to say that they did something. And I asked them what happened. And they told me they had no orders.
>
> "The police went by... but couldn't do anything." (Oscar, C&C)

---

[2] As we saw in the Introduction, this mixed pattern of police action (repression, passivity, participation) seemed to be present during the post-Katrina lootings.

"The police were right by our side, with their weapons. I told them: 'Brother, guard my store. What are you here for?' And his reply was: 'I can't, I can't, I can't. If I do something, I'll lose my job.'" (Pablo, C&C)

But the police were not totally passive. They did protect the gas station in El Cruce, for example, and some other specific stores at both sites with the zeal that other repressive forces reserved for big chain supermarkets (protection that seemed to have acted as a deterrent for some; as a neighbor from Lomas Verde said: "No, I didn't go to El Cruce.... What if I got a bullet?"). Vicente, who had two stores in El Cruce, with a police patrol car stationed at the larger of the two, notes that "the cops really helped us.... We would have not let the looters in anyway; we electrified the blinds. We were really prepared. And yet ... people still tried to break in." Without police protection, however, Vicente's other store was completely sacked.

Which stores were guarded? All the evidence that we were able to gather points to a pattern: Several store owners and employees mentioned that some stores paid for protection. In a way, the same logic that governs the protection of big chain supermarkets and the underprotection of small markets operates on a smaller scale in El Cruce and in C&C. Those who could afford it bought safety. A storekeeper told me his uncle (the owner of nearby butcher shop) paid for police protection in Moreno. An employee of a medium-size appliance store in El Cruce put it this way:

"There were cops right here, at the door, outside. At that moment, we asked the chief to please guard our store. We told him that we would later give him something. We gave him a TV set. And we gave a wristwatch to every cop. I guess that's why we were not attacked." (Augusto)

In Matanza, Gladys saw from across the street how the looters broke into her store: "I was alone, and I stayed in this and were thus spared from the destruction:

"I tried [to pay for protection] because half a block from here there's a supermarket that had a police car in front.... But when I closed my store I didn't have a single coin with me. I didn't have my wallet, not even my ID.... I know that in the next block they paid the police and the cops stayed there. I couldn't pay, I couldn't pay. And I guess some other people couldn't pay either. The police parked their cars in front of those stores that paid them."

Mauricio and his father tried, unsuccessfully, to defend their food store with an old rifle. "We shot twice... the bullets' marks are still in the ceiling." But most of the stuff was already gone when they got there: "It's sad to see so many years of hard work gone in 10 minutes.... It makes me very angry, but that's it, a bad memory, that's all." He does not know if some paid for police protection but does recognize that some stores in C&C were more protected than others because of differential acquaintanceship with local police agents:

"I don't know if someone paid, but there are people who are closer to the police, and they had police cars parked in front of their stores; we didn't. That day, if you walked a couple of blocks from our store you'd have seen two police cars parked in front of a couple of businesses; and nobody touched those stores."

Pablo, whose clothing store was devastated, also says that people paid for protection but not exactly to the police: "There are people who know who's *en la joda* [a codeword that refers to those who engage in criminal activity] and who told them: 'Brother, I'll give you 200 pesos and you guard my store... and nobody touched that store.' I wish I'd done that, but the whole thing caught me by surprise."[3]

Q: How come the stores on this side of the street were not looted? It's kind of surprising...

CRISTIAN: On this block... I don't know. Honestly, I don't know...

Q: With so many people looting on that side...

C: That's what I ask myself...

---

[3] This is consistent with many newspaper reports that noted that some stores throughout the Conurbano were protected by heavily armed residents, who were acquaintances of the store owners.

q: No idea...

c: No idea... I always ask myself that question, and I don't know. On this side, we were saved [*nos salvamos*], but I don't know why; in truth, I have no idea...

(Dialogue with Cristian, an employee of an appliance store in C&C, March 1, 2005)

In Matanza, there seems to be a more complicated pattern than in Moreno regarding who was attacked and who was saved, a pattern that is not simply reducible to "money pays for protection." Most store owners told us that, even if they do not know why, the stores on one side of the street (the Ciudad Evita side) were spared from violence, while those on the other side of the street (the San Alberto side) were devastated. We chose ten stores (five looted, five saved) and interviewed their owners. The five looted stores were on the San Alberto side. How could this pattern be explained? Store owners had dissimilar stories regarding this seemingly unexplainable configuration, but they ultimately recognized that they don't really know.

Community relations seem to have played an important role in channeling the violence: Those spared from the looting had lived in the neighborhood longer, had long-lasting ties with residents and local leaders, and lived adjacent to the stores – so they were able to better protect them. As Cristian, employee of a store that was not looted, puts it: "Most of the store owners on this side [Ciudad Evita] live there. The kids [who looted] know them; they all know each other. If I live in an alleyway, two houses from the store, I'm not going to loot that store." The spared side seems to be an older, more-connected side, whose members *work and live* there (as opposed to those who, on the San Alberto side, work but do not live there). Roxana, whose furniture store was not attacked, put it this way: "They, the looters, came *en masse*. They didn't approach this store because the neighbors here have known my father for thirty years, and the very same neighbors stood guard in front of the store." Her old father added from behind: "The looters all knew me."

Residence and the ensuing relationships mattered (as we saw) among the perpetrators of violence as well as among its potential victims. Oscar, who has lived in the neighborhood for the past thirty-two years and who has had a bicycle store since 1978, summarized how deep, trusting relationships worked well to avoid violence:

> o: The year 2001 was terrible for us. Thank God nothing happened to us [during the lootings] because...a little bit because of the knowledge that one has of the neighborhood, of the good and the bad. You know, they all know us...
>
> i: What do you mean by that?
>
> o: Well, you know, sometimes you have to live with God and with the Devil, side by side. Smile to whoever comes into the store, without discriminating, whether he is good or bad. We were on the sidewalks, watching how the other stores were looted, and they passed by and told me, 'Pajita [Oscar's nickname], you are next...'
>
> i: Just like that?
>
> o: Yep, just like that...
>
> i: And who told you that?
>
> o: All the criminals [*todos los delincuentes*]...those who loot are, for me, criminals. They didn't touch us, they didn't come into the store. Thank God.

"Thank God" and, one could add, "Thank relationships": The latter proved crucial in saving most of the people from violence. Some, like Oscar, were saved because of their familiarity with "the good and the bad" in the neighborhood. Others stood guard, weapon in hand, like Pascual with his five brothers in front of his store. That might have saved him, though it didn't save others. What seems to be specific to him is that, in addition to his weapons, he was armed with political links: "We knew a lot of *punteros*....They came to the store when they did fundraising....They brought us news [about the lootings]." This was what the minister of interior called, in a personal interview he gave me, "a network of fine gossiping" (which, as he confided, allowed them to find out about the upcoming lootings days in advance), and it served Pascual quite well. The lootings did not catch him by surprise.

Shopkeepers, both those who were looted and those who were spared, see a logical connection between the passivity of the police and the political character of the lootings. Their statements describing police inaction blend with assertions regarding the organized, preplanned, character of the lootings: The police did nothing because directives for their action or inaction "came from above."

Shopkeepers (and even some of the looters themselves) have little doubt about the political underpinnings of the lootings. Almost every single shopkeeper we interviewed in Moreno specifically mentioned a rally that was organized by the mayor as the trigger for the lootings, as the spark the started the fire. On December 19, the mayor of Moreno, Mariano West, himself a strongman within the Peronist Party, declared an economic emergency in his district and organized a rally to start in the main municipal building and head to the Plaza de Mayo to demand a change in economic policy. The mayor, together with party members, local officials, union leaders, and the Archbishop of Moreno, led thousands of citizens through the streets of Moreno, until the rally was stopped at the border of the Capital Federal by the national police. But, before it was dissolved, it passed through El Cruce. The heavy looting, most shopkeepers pointed out, began on the margins of this procession:

> "And the worst thing I remember is the caravan. It was organized by the mayor. He was at the head of it in a station wagon, and, following him, there were three blocks of people, cars, trucks, everything . . . and behind that . . . they were all looting. He instigated them to loot. All of the looters came with the mayor, breaking everything up, looting . . . " (Pedro)
>
> "The mayor came with a lot of people. . . . It was like a crazy thing but, that's how it is. We all know it was all political. It was all orchestrated. That's why this was a liberated zone." (Daniel)

Contrary to what national newspapers and the rally's organizers asserted at the time (*La Nación*, December 20), the *caravana* did not put an end to violence. As a local union leader, part of the caravan, admitted days later: "While many of us took part in the rally to demand jobs and a change of economic policy, behind us people were breaking windows and looting stores" (*Para Ud!* 2002:4). Almost every single storekeeper points to the rally as the moment at which the heavy looting began.

109

To them the fact that violence got under way at the margins of a rally organized by the mayor is the best proof of the political (i.e., organized, preplanned) character of the lootings:

> "Everybody around here was saying that it was all organized. I don't know anything about politics, but people were saying that the mayor prepared everything.... There was a caravan, and he brought all the people here..." (Mirta)

The caravan acted as a sign of the validation that the authorities gave to violent actions. It was hardly the only signal participants got. Looters and witnesses saw (and clearly remember) political authorities (the mayor, but also councilmen and other officials) at the looting scene; they also saw the police passively witnessing the sacking. To them this was a clear indication that their actions were not condemned. Furthermore, since *trusted* sources spread the news about imminent lootings (sources connected with municipal authorities like political brokers), looters believed that their actions enjoyed a certain degree of legitimacy. Certification by public authorities, another key causal mechanism in the generation of violence (Tilly 2003; McAdam, Tarrow, and Tilly 2001), was at work. Legitimating looters' actions was not an ex post facto result of the massive violence but worked in situ as the looting proceeded.

At the time, shopkeepers saw the caravan as an indication that the local government was fomenting the looting and would do nothing to stop it. Logically, it was for them a moment of terror, a moment in which they felt abandoned to the mercy of the looters. In very simple, candid terms, Mario, an old shopkeeper, puts it this way: "I don't understand much about politics, but it was all political. Because if the police don't do anything, if the government doesn't do anything... that means it's all organized, it's all politics." Whether they were looted or not, shopkeepers have little doubt about what initiated the lootings.

Brokers in the Gray Zone of Politics

Far from being "outsider organizers," brokers are, as we saw in Chapter 2, deeply embedded in the everyday life of the urban poor in Argentina. They are part and parcel of daily community living; they also take part in

110

less-ordinary actions – the lootings being one such but hardly the only examples. Two recent cases of land squatting in urban settings further illustrate the location of brokers in a nebulous area and their activities, sometimes promoting squatting, at other times forcing evictions from squatted lands. These cases also illustrate the (usually hidden) connections that tie together party activists and members of the police force.

Early on the morning of April 2, 2004, hundreds of poor persons invaded an unfinished housing complex in the northwest city of Santiago del Estero. A day before, the federal government ordered the intervention of the provincial administration after a series of corruption scandals in which the governor, the local caudillo Carlos Juarez, and his wife and vice-governor, Nina, were presumably involved. The couple presided over one of the most resilient patronage-based political machines in the country: The *Juarizmo* has ruled the province, formally or informally, for the last fifty years. The official sent by the federal administration to head the "*intervención*" soon found out that it was not going to be easy to deal with the Juarezes – even if they were in jail, as they had been since April 1 – and to dismantle a political machine that had been long in the making. The land invasion was one of the many attempts that Juarez's faction would make to try to disrupt the new administration. According to many accounts (*Clarín, Página12, La Nación*), *punteros juaristas* fomented the invasion. The new occupants told reporters that the provincial police (by then, still under the control of the Juarezes) left the place unguarded "because Nina gave the order to do so" (*Clarín.com* April 3, 2004). Another source reported that brokers working for the Juarezes created a "liberated zone" around it.

Like the invasion in Santiago, squatter settlements around the world (occupations of land or buildings without the explicit permission of the owner) provide examples of the intersection of partisan politics and collective action. As a recent report from the United Nations Human Settlements Programme (2003:82, my emphasis) states: "Although the initial settlements may have been the result of the authorities turning a blind eye, particularly during the immediate post-independence inflow of migrants to the cities of Asia and Africa, squatting became a large and profitable business, often carried out with the active, if *clandestine*, participation of politicians, policemen, and privateers of all kinds."

Party brokers, the example in Santiago shows, instigate squatting. Party brokers, the following example demonstrates, can also be at the other end of action: violently forcing evictions. What happened was this:

> Last Monday, 35-year-old Julio Medina was putting up his house on a squatters' plot of land in Berazategui (in the state of Buenos Aires) when he saw four plainclothes policemen coming towards him, escorted by several cars. While a group of uniformed police occupied the side of the street, the ones not wearing uniforms entered the settlement and removed the families that were there using physical force and displaying their guns. Medina told *Página12* that "One of my neighbors asked the cops to show him the judicial order to vacate, but they arrested him."... The four plainclothes policemen destroyed the metal and wood shacks. The local police precinct later took custody of the land. Nestor Rojas, head of the *Federación de Tierra y Vivienda* of Berazategui denounced these actions: "The police came with some Peronist *punteros* to beat the people here, with no judicial order. They violently vacated the land, and then they began to intimidate the people.... The gang [*la patota*] that destroyed the houses in the squatter settlement, Rojas says, "came with Jorge Osán, who has the rank of municipal delegate."[4]

The preceding examples show brokers carrying out different sorts of gray zone actions. What exactly were brokers from the Peronist Party doing among the looting crowds on December 18 and 19 in Matanza and Moreno? Let me present two contrasting views and then move to the sites of the lootings and offer the perspectives of store owners and participants. To foreshadow, hardly anyone doubts the *punteros'* presence – as the lootings were waning, some people, like grassroots leader D'Elia (cited in the next section), were already publicly voicing their opinions about their damaging actions. Years later, many are still convinced that *punteros* were indeed "there," among the looting crowds. When it comes to stating exactly what they were doing there, matters become much more disputed. Let's see.

D'Elia's View

Luis D'Elia is the leader of the *Federación de Tierra y Vivienda*, a grassroots organization that, during 2000 and 2001, coordinated some of the largest

---

[4] From Vales (2003b).

and longest road blockades in protest against the De La Rua administration. He is one of the best known *piquetero* leaders in the country. He is now a member of the House of Representatives from the province of Buenos Aires and is part of a broad coalition supporting President Kirchner's administration. In the early 1980s, D'Elia was an active member of the land squatter movement and a member of *Humanismo y Liberación* (a left faction within the Christian Democratic Party, where he and I met). He still lives in El Tambo, one of the squatter settlements in La Matanza that he helped to organize. On the night of December 20, he went to a widely watched TV program (*PuntoDoc*) and, live from the studio, denounced the Peronist Party, Governor Ruckauf, and Secretary of Security Alvarez. *Punteros* from the party and top officials from the Peronist administration were, according to D'Elia, the masterminds behind the lootings. To what purpose? To provide the impetus for a coup d'etat against President De La Rua. D'Elia is hardly alone in this view; it is a widely shared belief among both looters and the looted. I had read D'Elia's statements regarding the lootings in newspapers and in a book that devotes an entire chapter to these episodes (Bonasso 2002), but I wanted to hear his description of the events first-hand. We met for about two hours, and we talked a couple of times over the phone. By the end of the interview, which took place in the FTV offices in downtown Buenos Aires, the room was filled with D'Elia's *compañeros* who volunteered additional accounts and interpretations. In the following transcription, I decided to preserve my questions as they were formulated, several iterations of the same topic, because they reflect the ways in which the episodes were described and (mis)understood (by me, that is).

D: I saw this coming . . . during the six months before the lootings, I woke up asking myself: "Is today the day?" We knew that it was going to explode . . .

J: You went to the judge to accuse the *punteros* from the Peronist Party of being the main actors behind all the episodes, right?

D: That's right. But nothing happened in court. *Punteros* did two sorts of things: some of them directed the looting. For lootings to occur there has to be a liberated territory. So, they moved the police away. And then

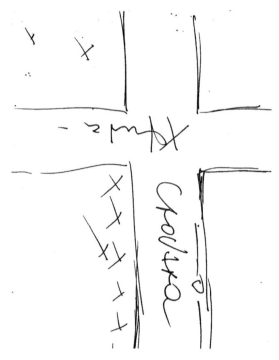

Figure 7. Drawing of D'Elia's View.

they recruited people saying that they were going to loot. They did this from the *Unidades Básicas*...

J: Do you think that's what happened?

D: It's not that I think so. I saw it. May I invite two *compañeros* into the room?

D'Elia calls in Pepino and Rubén, who were in an adjacent room and who are his neighbors and fellow activists in La Matanza. He then asks for a piece of paper and draws the picture shown in Figure 7.

D: The people from the *Unidades Básicas* populated the area of Crovara and Cristianía with their own people [marked in his drawing with Xs], as if they had been recruited for such a day. They moved the police away; the police usually have their patrols stationed here. That day, the police disappeared. And, at a certain time, they hurled the people against the stores...

114

J: When you say they recruited people...

D: I know *compañeros* who were recruited...

J: And did they know there would be no police in the area?

D: Obviously...when you create such a vanguard, then everybody wants to go. Once the thing started, everybody got hooked. Even my neighbor went with his cart and picked up half a cow!

D'Elia has an intuitive view of what collective action scholars call the "creation of opportunities." He also has a keen analytic eye that distinguishes something that many collective violence scholars (myself included) have trouble differentiating: the creation of opportunities and how those very same opportunities are taken advantage of.

J: It is as if the actions of the police and the actions of the *punteros* were coordinated...

D: No doubt about it. There were police helicopters flying over the area, there were cars with *punteros* in them going around. Everything was coordinated. Entire areas were liberated. Vanguards, small groups, were recruited. *Once you put together 300 people to loot, you will soon have 10,000. Brokers moved the police away and called the first looters. Those first hundreds generated the devastation that followed.* (my emphasis)

When I interviewed D'Elia, he was being prosecuted for the occupation of a police precinct in La Boca (he was later absolved). With a group of FTV activists, he had occupied the police headquarters in protest against police complicity in the assassination of an FTV militant. During the course of our conversation, he contrasted that occupation with the lootings:

D: The lootings...this is a theme about which someone, at some point, will have to tell the truth. Because it was a coup d'etat. De La Rua was an asshole, an *inservible* [useless person] with whom we [at the FTV] have two million differences. We were on the opposition. But this was not the way [to get rid of him]. Chaos can never be a good way. This was a coup, and it was prepared from above. And now the guys who did this are around [i.e., in active political life]. And I am the worst of all, because I went to a police precinct because a *compañero* was killed. And they devastated a big part of the Conurbano. They destroyed the lives of many shopkeepers.

115

By now the room was filled with other FTV members, and everyone was recollecting an anecdote from those days. I looked at D'Elia and asked:

J: But, Luis, all this sounds like a conspiracy...

D: [everybody laughing] Yes, that's what it was...

J: You are laughing but...

X [smiling]: You can't believe it, can you?

D: Those who looted were residents from around. They were from there. *Punteros* also carried out a psychological action. The night after the lootings, they went around in an old truck, telling people that neighbors from one area were coming to loot: "They are coming from El Tambo to attack the barrio Don Juan." And so the people from Don Juan were all in the streets waiting for the El Tambo residents. First they looted, they devastated the commercial strip, and then they created that mess. That night I was invited to *Punto Doc* (TV program), and it took me three hours to get there [usually a forty-five-minute ride]. There were barricades everywhere, people were terrified.

The Official/Peronist Viewpoint

Aníbal Fernández is a man at the heart of Peronism. He knows the party inside out. He has been the mayor of Quilmes, a major district of the Conurbano; then he was minister of labor during the Ruckauf administration in the province of Buenos Aires, and he is now minister of the interior – among his many tasks he commands the federal police. We talked for an hour-and-a-half at the Government Palace. I have never interviewed an official as high in the public administration as he was; his level of concentration in our conversation – with two TV sets on, one radio news station playing, and three cell phones constantly ringing ("Being on top of the information is power," he told me) – was simply outstanding.

The one (and probably only) commonality he has with D'Elia is that both of them saw the lootings coming way before they occurred. "A big mess was in the making," he told me, and "we tried to calm things down, by distributing food – we gave away like a million dollars worth of food – and by paying the unemployment subsidies in advance. But we were doing this at the state level; meanwhile the federal government was rolling back, they were cutting, cutting, cutting... and a huge

116

mess was coming [*y se venía el quilombo*]." How did they know about impending collective violence? "We have a *sistema of alcahuetería fina* [a system of fine gossiping] that told us that lootings were coming . . . days before we knew it." What for D'Elia is a network of information that flows from top to bottom (commands were, according to him, given from the higher echelons of the Peronist Party to the low-level *punteros* to organize the violence), for the minister is a network that transmits information in the other direction (letting officials know what's going on at the grassroots level).

Minister Fernandez recalls that on the nineteenth, he met with Governor Ruckauf, Secretary of Security Alvarez, and the Peronist mayors of the Conurbano in the offices of the Banco Provincia (State Bank) in downtown Buenos Aires. "We decided two things: avoid killings and repair the damage after it was done" (killings by the police were indeed avoided, but damages were never repaired – not a single store owner was indemnified for the destruction in spite of the government's promises). Aníbal Fernandez recounts that, in that meeting, the general agreement among Peronist leaders was that the general commotion in Buenos Aires was a sort of "creation" of the "intelligence services" (commanded by the Federal Administration) to make Ruckauf's government collapse (Ruckauf was a likely candidate to succeed the then very unpopular De La Rua). The minister of the interior agrees with the then–secretary of security, Alvarez: The lootings were not a conspiracy of the Peronists to make the Alianza government collapse. If anything, it was the other way around. Alvarez told me that federal intelligence services "should have known" about the coming lootings – "In my experience they are not that dumb [*no son tan pelotudos*]. . . . So, if they knew it, why didn't they do something to prevent them? Because they were conspiring against Ruckauf." Both Alvarez and Fernandez denied *punteros'* involvement in the lootings, but with caution. On one hand, Fernandez told me:

> "Maybe there are things about the lootings that I don't know . . . but I don't have evidence. There has not been a move coming from our [Peronist] government to generate such a thing. Had there been leaders behind the lootings, we could have identified them. But there's no videotape showing *punteros* in action. It wouldn't be

difficult to find them; for two hundred pesos you can find anybody in this country. I don't think there were *punteros* organizing the lootings.... Mind you, that's what I know.... Maybe there are things I don't know." On the other hand, Alvarez told me, "I would not be able to categorically deny the presence of *punteros* among the looting crowds. But they were there because they are neighbors, they live there. Where do you think the Peronist ballots [before and during the elections] are distributed? In those small stores [that were sacked]; that's why they were there. There was not a Peronist conspiracy behind the lootings. There might have been a *puntero* from the Menemist faction [a faction led by former President Menem] involved. But it was not a maneuver coming from the Peronist Party.... True, this was hardly spontaneous. Who started it? I would like to know."

He ends his assertions regarding the role of the Peronist Party in the lootings with a curious general agreement with his accuser D'Elia: "A small group set the fire ... then many got involved."

The Views from Below and from Inside

Shopkeepers' descriptions of looters' actions are fragmented for a reason. They were inside the stores (some reported having stayed in for five days), trying to guard them as best as they could: some by arming themselves, others by connecting the metal blinds to high-voltage wires, others by reinforcing the doors. All of them were terrified at the prospect of being attacked and cannot provide good accounts of what was going on among the looters. From what they saw at the time, and what they heard days later, some were able to point at the existence of a certain level of coordination among the looters and at the presence of political brokers among the crowds:

"You could see the people were recruited or, I don't know ... in agreement." (Vicente, Moreno)

"There were guys directing the thing.... They said, 'You go there, you there ...'" (Pablo, Moreno)

"Seeing so many people took us by surprise.... But they [the orga-
nizers] were not surprised...they had everything prepared. They
communicated with cell phones..." (Norma, Moreno)

"*Punteros* [organized this], *punteros* directed by the mayor. He told
them which area they were in charge of." (Mirta, Moreno)

The most adamant account of the presence of *punteros* and their actions
comes from Pablo and his mother Susana whose store in La Matanza
was destroyed in "a second."

SUSANA: Stores were marked...

PABLO: Stores were marked. Here there was a political move, a political move that everybody knows. Not a single store on Ciudad Evita's
side was touched [i.e., looted]; the stores on the San Alberto's side
were destroyed. That means that there were *punteros* coordinating
the whole thing, [telling people] which store should be attacked and
which store should not.... *Punteros* had weapons. I was with my old
man outside, and we were guarding our source of income [*estábamos
cuidando nuestra fuente de ingreso*]. It took us a whole life to have something like this. It's awful to lose it in one second. We confronted the
people: "Listen, if we serve you every day, we are like you guys...."
And the people retreated, but then a *puntero* ordered them: "Come
on, come on, come on...," and the *punteros* told me and my old
man, "Move away or you are gone [*salí porque sos boleta*]." And that's
when we moved away, and when it happened. In a second, nothing
was left.

There is little doubt that Peronist brokers were indeed involved in the
looting episodes that took place both in El Cruce and in C&C. Investigative journalists reporting from Moreno and La Matanza stated this,
and my own research has found evidence of their presence. But, after
dozens of interviews and informal conversations, I lack strong evidence
to prove Susana's and Pablo's claims regarding "marked" stores and *punteros* openly directing the actions (with the exception of D'Elia's testimony cited earlier and a few other store owners who told me similar stories). The accounts are too contradictory: Some participants, bystanders,
and shopkeepers saw – as did Susana and Pablo – *punteros* in the midst of

119

the looting crowds doing something more than simply looking. Others say they didn't see any. Following are comments from a sample of those who, in Matanza, saw organizers (residents usually do not use the term "*punteros*") among the attackers:

> "Maybe, yes [there were organizers], because of politics. They organized because they were the ones who first got inside. They said, 'Here, we are going to sack this one.' And they were in command. And after them, came the rest of the people; but they went in first. . . . Politics is the worst thing." (Domingo)

> "I went with my mum to see what was going on. . . . It was a disaster. People are not to be blamed [for what happened], because they were directed. . . . There was one who gave directions, 'Let's break into that store.' There were people who devoted themselves simply to breaking things; but they didn't get inside the stores. They simply broke the gates so that people could enter. They had crowbars in their hands. They broke the gates and tore them apart." (Elizabeth)

> "Everything was organized. They carried walkie-talkies. . . . Five or six leaders were the ones who moved the whole thing." (Cristian, who stayed inside his store during the lootings. The store was not attacked.)

> "There were organizers among the looters. People with cell phones . . . telling the rest where to go, which gate to break." (Pascual, who stayed, armed, inside his store. The store was not attacked.)

> "It was organized . . . because someone would say, 'Let's go there,' and everybody followed; and then, 'Let's go to this other place,' and everybody went." (Noelia, whose store was looted)

> "It was planned. Some guys said, 'Here, first, then here.'" (Pablo, whose store was looted)

How do we settle the disputed brokers' role? During the course of my fieldwork I toyed with the idea of becoming a detective in pursuit of the elusive broker – without much success. Even if they did what many people said they had done, they would hardly admit it four years later. How exactly were brokers involved? Although some Peronist brokers might have promoted the looting by recruiting followers, their main action (at least, the one for which I have the best evidence) seemed to have been the following: They spread the news regarding the upcoming (looting) opportunity. As Delia, herself a powerful Peronist broker in Lomas Verde, matter-of-factly told me: "We [the members of the Peronist Party] knew about the lootings beforehand, around 1 A.M. We knew that there was going to be a looting. We were told about it and we passed the information along to our people [among the members of the party]." Different from the claims for food organized by picketers at the beginning of the looting week, Peronist brokers did not take their followers to the stores, nor could they control their actions. However, they did do something crucial: They passed the word about the location of the looting – simply by spreading rumors throughout the community that *saqueos* were "coming" at the crossroads of Crovara and Cristianía in La Matanza and in El Cruce in Moreno, places populated not by large chain supermarkets, but by small retail stores. These were "safe places" to loot – police would not be present and, if present, would not act. How did brokers and people in general know about police future (in)activity? In part, they assumed it because news about upcoming lootings was coming from above, from well-connected state actors; in part, they experienced it on site when they saw that the infamous *Bonaerense* was, in the words of the broker-turned-looter, "worse than us, they were the ones who took most of the things . . . and when we were inside El Chivo [a devastated supermarket in El Cruce], *they even told us where to escape so that we wouldn't get in trouble.*"

Even though flyers inviting people to attack supermarkets did indeed circulate before the lootings (as mentioned in the Introduction), and although there are reports that say that brokers "took" prospective looters to the sites, it seems to me that the role of brokers was less straightforward. Through their networks, brokers publicized information (or simply gossip) concerning the upcoming distribution of food in local supermarkets. But they were not acting as an organized group. Some brokers I interviewed told me (and I have every reason to believe them) that during the lootings they were told by their superiors in the local government to "try to calm things down." Mabel, another prominent broker in Lomas Verde, told me that "in the municipality they told us to be careful because there were people looting in El Cruce. They called me from the municipal government and asked me to tell people not to go to El Cruce." Juan and Yolanda, Peronist brokers from the Barrio BID, told us that "during the lootings, the municipal government gave orders to try to hold people [*contenerlos*], to keep them in their homes." Other brokers, from the same party, passed the information along and encouraged their followers to go. Given their own reputation as food-providers, residents of poverty enclaves acted on this information that was broadcast by brokers and began gathering in front of these stores. With hundreds and sometimes thousands of desperate people believing in the imminent dispersal of food gathered in front of unguarded stores, minor contingencies (and the actions of petty thieves and, maybe, yes, some other *punteros*) then determined the unfolding or not of collective violence. Together with the validation that public authorities gave to violence (validation that we saw at work during the rally organized by the mayor in Moreno, in the passive presence of municipal officials, and in the permissive actions of the police at the looting sites), we can then detect the working of another mechanism that is deemed central in episodes of collective violence – signaling spirals (McAdam, Tarrow, and Tilly 2001). Before and during the lootings, brokers communicated the location of targets, the presence or absence of police, and thus the feasibility of risky practices.

It was not easy to figure out the actual steps through which one resident became a looter. For example, how did Marta, who that morning was cleaning her house and preparing lunch for her daughter, find herself breaking into Daniel's store half an hour later? Signaling was here crucial. Friends and neighbors, in cooperation with political brokers, indicated to each other (a) when lootings were about to start and (b) where it was safe to loot. Signaling basically comprised (a) protection from potential repressive action (as many a resident told me, "I didn't go through that street because neighbors told me the cops were there") and (b) logistics (as participants told me, some places were spared damage because they had heavy gates or private security). This mutual signaling was carried out on the spur of the moment. We were repeatedly informed: "There were a lot of people in the streets, saying that looting was taking place at...." Different from other one-day riots (e.g., the one that shocked the otherwise peaceful city of Santiago del Estero in December 1993), signaling did not include explicit negotiations among looters or between looters and looted. The kind of evidence I was able to collect for Santiago del Estero (Auyero 2003) – where rioters did talk about their future targets, considered alternatives, and sometimes made collective decisions based on the owner of the property and its characteristics – is absent for Moreno and La Matanza. There are no indications that looters, for example, met at a certain place beforehand and/or "decided" what the next target was going to be.

The interactions between the behavior of the state police, the tacit approval that authorities gave to the first lootings, and the brokers' continuing spread of information created the opportunity to loot. Given the critical situation in which residents were living, the past experience of lootings in the area, the closeness of a busy commercial strip, and the simultaneous existence of lootings in other parts of the province and of the country (about which they were informed by radio and television), it did not take much for residents of poor enclaves such as Lomas Verde and BID to take advantage of this opportunity.

Actors have competing explanations and/or interpretations of the same actions: As we saw, some interpret the presence of brokers as proof of their role as "instigators" of collective violence. Others explain that very same presence differently: They were there, "because they live around here," "to calm things down," "to find out what was going on." Akin to Wilkinson's portrait of some Indian political parties (Wilkinson 2004), many – grassroots leaders, store owners, neighbors – believe that the Peronist Party gave specific *instructions* that *caused* the mayhem. One prominent activist, known for his leadership in one of the largest organizations of the unemployed workers, told me:

> "Yesterday I went to a meeting with several mayors of Buenos Aires. One of them, took me aside and told me: 'You know, in this very same place, on December 2001, [then Governor] Ruckauf told us [members of the Peronist Party] to make a big mess in the Conurbano.'"

How do I assess these competing explanations/interpretations? What is the relationship between the massive collective violence and the interests of the parties involved? All the available evidence (my own and

123

that culled by journalists) points toward some sectors of the Peronist Party (mainly those allied with former Governor Ruckauf) as the most important groups "behind" the makings of the lootings in Moreno and La Matanza. The actions of these sectors of the Peronist Party might not be the ultimate cause of the lootings in the country as a whole (there are many places in which lootings did occur and there is no evidence of the presence of Peronist brokers). However, given that (a) Peronist brokers were highly visible in places where looting was massive, most damaging, and highly consequential in terms of the political impacts of looting (i.e., the Conurbano) and (b) government officials in the state of Buenos Aires, who are also members of the Peronist Party, prevented the police from acting once the lootings broke out, it is not far-fetched to assert that sectors of the Peronist Party promoted the violence. They did so not necessarily to overthrow the government but to display their disruptive power. Peronists' final goal might not have been a coup, but they surely wanted to demonstrate their collective might. They were doing politics by other (violent) means.

Together with police passivity, the presence of brokers then highlights the existence of a gray zone of politics that, central during the lootings, illustrates the existing continuities between routine and contentious politics. There is no way of knowing if the gray zone of politics (where the obscure and obscured actions of local politicos, grassroots brokers, and cops meet and mesh in seemingly coordinated ways) is the ultimate cause of the lootings. The massive violence that took place in December 2001, however, throws light on the existence of an area of politics in which the dichotomies that the literature on collective action still hold dear seem to collapse: repressive forces that don't suppress violence and that give a hand to looters and/or turn a blind eye to their damage-making actions, state actors who seemingly foment violence while rallying for peace, political brokers who regularly conduct patronage, but at least some of whom instigate their followers to break into unguarded stores. In the whole process, rumors – fast and furious gossiping about the goods that are accessible at the looting sites and about the absence of police – were central. Brokers and police agents were, apparently, their main source. Let us now look at this peculiar form of communication and its impact on the development *and demise* of collective violence.

The Double Life of Rumors

As mentioned previously, rumors were crucial at the onset of the lootings. They "informed" residents that food was being distributed by certain supermarkets and, in doing so, created the conditions for collective violence. Rumors also let shopkeepers know that something was in the offing. As lootings were occurring, rumors rapidly circulated among looters regarding impending police action and among shopkeepers concerning future targets. Rumors also multiplied toward the end of the lootings but had an opposite effect: They seem to have prevented further looting. In what follows I examine this other side of rumors.[5]

In his analysis of the creation and functions of rumors, Ralph Rosnow (1988:16, my emphasis) points out that:

> rumor construction is a way of promulgating new schemes of coordination when we undergo a *derangement in our way of life*. When aspects of a system are *"out of joint"* with one another, i.e. when there is a *strain* in an essential institutional structure, we become apprehensive and actively seek each other's support and perspective concerning what is happening.... Through repetition of rumors, mutual expectations become fixed and new ways of *coping with perceived threats to the existing order attain clarity and coherence of purpose.*

A key motivating force in the construction of rumor is the pursuit of meaning; through rumor transmission, we seek information, and we restructure our perceptions in order to cope with an important but ambiguous situation in which we find ourselves. Key factors in the rapid generation and spread of rumors, Rosnow asserts, are personal anxiety, general uncertainty, and credulity.

The rumormongering that flowed throughout the Conurbano on December 20 and 21 proves Rosnow right. As reported in the press and in my interviews, uncertainty about what was going to happen next and anxiety about further violence became widespread among residents of low-income neighborhoods and shopkeepers. Rumors began to spread

---

[5] Journalistic reports on post-Katrina lootings (cited in the Introduction) highlight this latter aspect of rumors. A version of "you loot, I shoot" operated in both Moreno and La Matanza, prompting small-store owners to arm themselves and to guard their property.

like fire, and a sense of trepidation became widespread. By providing "information" that enabled residents and shopkeepers to suspend their disbelief, rumors spurred them to take immediate action – thus allowing them to cope with the situation by seeking to control it.

At the time of the episodes, Canadian anthropologist Lindsay DuBois was living in Billinghurst, a working-class neighborhood in the district of San Martin that was the site of heavy looting activity. She writes (2002:4):

> The night of the 19th–20th, I awoke to the sound of firecrackers and barking dogs. When I looked out the window, I saw fires burning in the intersections at both ends of our block. Daniel, my husband, went out to investigate, and returned looking for wood scraps and other fuel for the fires. When I asked what was happening, he told me neighbors had been warned that hordes of people were coming to invade our houses, and that the large firecrackers were being set off to wake up everyone so that they would be on the alert. In response to my disbelief, Daniel's rushed answer was he had to seem to support neighbors who set themselves up for an all-night vigil tending the fires. Those of us inside did not get much more sleep. A brief tour of the neighborhood in the morning showed signs that similar fires had been set at virtually every intersection in the neighborhood. The bonfires and vigils continued for two more nights.

Bonfires and barricades in poor and low-income neighborhoods, set up by residents to defend their few possessions from the presumed attacks of angry looters rampaging nearby, were widely reported in the press.

> The neighborhood can't sleep and is on guard [*El vecindario no puede conciliar el sueño y vigila*].
> Nightmare. That is what the neighbors of the barrio San José, in Temperley, had to live through at dawn.... It was sheer terror. Gunshots, barricades, fire, nervousness and panic. Fear. They were coming from "Fuerte Apache," from "Don Orione," from "Dos de Abril,"... nobody was certain about where the looters were coming from.... Many decided to arm themselves and wait. They took turns mounting guard... there was no other solution, because they only got the answering machine when they called the local police precinct. Fernanda (a neighbor) assured me that "We were told that people are sacking homes in Claypole [a

nearby district], and that they are coming toward us. The neighbors set up barricades because it is said that the looters are coming in two buses. My family hooked the fence of my house to high voltage. We agreed that we will stay awake and alert everybody if something happens. The same thing is going on in my boyfriend's barrio ... something strange is happening." (*Crónica*, December 22, 2001:7)

Always a good source of police information and a widely read newspaper among low-income groups, *Crónica* (December 21, 2001:12) reported that "early this morning [December 21] fear was widespread among residents of the Conurbano. They armed themselves and set up guards because they were afraid their homes would be sacked ... Afflicted residents from diverse localities, using sticks, cudgels, knives, fire-locks, and guns, firmly gripped by men and their sons, mounted guard since dawn in front of their homes because of the 'imminent attack' of 'hordes' of looters who were coming for the 'shantytowns'." In Merlo, an officer from the local police precinct, observed that hundreds of neighbors were awaiting "the enemy" by tending fires on the corners of their barrio. The leader of one of the largest picketer organizations said that in a neighborhood of La Matanza they "had to put up barricades so that the thieves [*chorros*] couldn't go through" (*Crónica*, December 21, 2001:12). The same newspaper quoted residents of the Conurbano who were worried about buses filled with "people from the shantytown" who were presumably attacking homes and setting them on fire. The next day, and as the lootings were slowly coming to an end, *Crónica* matter-of-factly reported the "proliferation of an alarming psychosis due to the lootings" and informed its readers that throughout Buenos Aires residents were still manning barricades to protect their barrios from attackers. Reporting from La Matanza, Laura Vales wrote in *Página12* (Vales 2001) that in squatter settlements and shantytowns people manned barricades to stop those from other barrios from coming to loot. Luis D'Elia told her: "Many went to the barricades with sticks, knives, and guns."

In the many conversations we had with residents of Lomas Verde and Barrio BID, there were several discrepant points of view (some said they saw organizers among the looting crowds, others didn't; some pointed to a "looting vanguard," others didn't; etc.). But on the subject of the rumors during the night after the lootings, there is a single, common account. They all remember how "chilling," how "frightening" that night was, with the impending invasion from other poor barrios. Let me quote a sample of the testimonies from the Barrio BID:

"We closed everything because news went around [*se había corrido la bolilla*] that they were going to loot the private houses, that they were going to break into them. [...] The same people who looted the grocery stores were coming from everywhere, from San Alberto, from all over. [...] They were coming to loot. Many people went around the neighborhood in trucks, telling people to close their doors, to put locks everywhere." (Andrea)

"Afterwards, people said that looters were coming from Fuerte Apache, from Villa Palito, they were coming to sack our homes." (Patricia)

"Around 4 A.M., everybody said that they were coming from other barrios. And so we started to secure our home. We started to block the alleyways, with sticks and with whatever we had at hand. Every neighbor did that. Those who had weapons carried them. Me and my husband did not have a gun; my husband stayed outside with a big stick. We didn't sleep that night." (Leonor)

"The night after the lootings was terrible, because it was said that gangs from other places were coming here. My poor daughter was feeling very bad...her stomach; she couldn't leave the bathroom...that's how scared she was. [...] The kids, who are usually petty thieves, were then protecting the neighborhood; they stayed outside saying, 'This is my area, and nobody will go through it.'" (Iris)

"The alleyways were closed off with sticks and parts of trees. Everybody had a gun. They were standing on the roofs. Nobody slept. There was this tension because it was said they were coming from San Pete, Puerta de Hierro, from the shantytowns." (Mario)

"We were up all night! They were coming, and then they were not coming! People from Laferrere, from Celina, from San Alberto...they were coming to loot [...] It was very tense. That night, on every corner, men stood outside. Women stayed inside.

They were all armed, with sticks, with rifles. [. . .] It was chilling. The only good thing is that the whole neighborhood got together to defend itself." (Mariana)

The attacks never materialized. Juan José Alvarez, then–Secretary of Security of Buenos Aires, informed the public at a press conference on December 22 that "police precincts received close to 5,000 calls concerning possible lootings in private homes, but in every case they were false alarms." *Crónica* itself said that, having checked with several police precincts of the Conurbano, they did not have information about lootings in private homes. What was going on?

That rumors were swiftly circulating is hardly disputed. Every newspaper remarked on this fact, and my own interviews confirmed it. The evidence is more controversial, however, when it comes to their source. *Crónica*, for one, pointed out that the general psychosis was "produced by a sinister campaign of unknown origin" (*Crónica*, December 22, 2001:6) and reported the repeated disclaimers made by police officers concerning lootings of entire neighborhoods and/or private homes. Based on her own conversations with her neighbors in Billinghurst, Lindsay DuBois thinks differently. She points toward the police as the main source of rumormongering and speculates about its main impact. The rumors of "invading hordes" had, she asserts, a demobilizing effect, keeping people at home, defending their barrios, thus preventing further looting. Her view dovetails with the diagnosis made by the most detailed journalistic report on the lootings (Young et al. 2002). Describing the actions of *La Bonaerense*, reporters from *Clarín* asserted that the police:

> broke out of its passivity with one precise objective: to impose fear, sometimes wearing uniforms, other times in plainclothes. The technique was simple and effective. Policemen went to a barrio and told neighbors that people from a nearby barrio were coming to rob. They advised neighbors to arm themselves, to stay awake, to tend fires and barricades on the corners, and to lock themselves at home. . . . In Lomas they told residents that invaders were coming from Camino Negro. In Avellaneda, cops in uniform announced that thieves were coming from Villa Tranquila. . . . In La Matanza, policemen were spreading the news about an invasion of Villegas by residents of El Tambo. . . . Such a level of coordination, at a similar time and throughout the Conurbano, could only

129

be explained by a decisive action of the chief of the police department [*jefatura*]. . . . Officially, there were no attacks by a barrio on another barrio, not of the poor against the rich, not even of the poor against the poor. There were false alarms, [it was] an intelligence operation."

Then–Secretary of Security Alvarez confided to me that the source might have been the police. His own daughter, Pilar, called him on the night of the twentieth desperately crying because "the looters were going to attack my home." He sent a special force to protect his house (and to calm down his daughter), but "it was nothing. Rumors were going like crazy which proved that this was the work of professionals." In his own, straightforward style he told me: "The message was the same. Stay at home, or they [the looters] will break your ass."

Rumors quickly spread at the beginning and at the end of the looting week. But the outcome of the rumors was quite different at these two moments in time. Rumors fostered lootings but also contributed to their demise. If DuBois and *Clarín*'s investigative team are correct (and, based on interviews with officials and other journalists, I find their accounts highly plausible[6]), we can thus conclude that the police were at both ends of the collective violence that traumatized the Conurbano during December: They were there as creators of opportunities to loot and as the actors who closed those same opportunities. In stopping collective violence with a combination of selective escalation of repression and rapid circulation of rumors, they proved themselves to be a key factor in its making.

---

[6] In their paper describing the memories of the 1989 lootings, Neufeld and Cravino (2003) assert that rumors concerning attacks on neighborhoods by mobs of looters were also running rampant at the time. They quote José, a resident of San Miguel (a district neighboring Moreno), who remembers that "[i]n each block there were 8 to 10 guys with guns, machetes, knives, tending a fire. I went to the nearby shantytown [and asked the people there] if they were coming to attack our neighborhood. 'No' [a shanty resident replied], 'you are the ones coming to attack us.'" (2003:8). Newspapers at the time also report the quick diffusion of rumors about invasions of shantytown dwellers. José also points to the police as the source of these rumors: "The intelligence service told the police to go around telling people to stay at home because people from other barrios were coming and they would loot, burn homes, and rape and kill people. I went around like crazy, screaming, 'Women and kids get inside, the men should stay outside because people from other neighborhoods are going to sack us!'" (Neufeld and Cravino 2003:8).

5

Making Sense of Collective Violence

The historical facts, of course, are known by everyone. . . . But facts do not make history; facts do not even make events. Without meaning attached, and without understanding of causes and connections, a fact is an isolate particle of experience, is reflected light without a source, planet with no sun, star without constellation, constellation beyond galaxy, galaxy outside the universe – fact is nothing.

Russell Banks, *Affliction*

And it was horrible, horrible . . . (crying) something not to be remembered.

Gladys, owner of a looted stored in La Matanza

Field Notes, July 26, 2005
Today was a day of extremes; social, symbolic, political, and economic extremes. I'm still trying to make sense of "the trip" – the journey that took me, early in the morning, from my place in Chacarita to the Government Palace in downtown Buenos Aires (the "Pink House" as it is locally known) and ended by noon at Irma's house in La Matanza. I spent close to two hours speaking with the current minister of the interior, Anibal Fernandez, about the year 2001 in general and the lootings in particular. Hours later I was having lunch with Irma, talking about her current, difficult life and about the 2001 *saqueos*. I ended up the day talking frantically with my former advisor about the kind of personal and professional habitus that is required to adjust, promptly, one's body, gestures, and speech in order to somehow succeed in carrying out meaningful conversations in both places.

Irma lived in the Barrio BID when the lootings took place. On December 19th, she was cleaning the sidewalks when she saw her neighbors running toward Crovara and Cristianía shouting: "*Están saqueando, están saqueando*" ("They are looting, they are looting"). That day, she had seen on TV that similar episodes had taken place at the French-owned supermarket Auchan, in nearby La Tablada – but it was a "partial looting," she told me, "because they had private security." When her son, Bebe (then 19 years old), saw all the people going to C&C, he rushed, too. Irma, worried, went after him. She tried, unsuccessfully, to persuade him to come back: "Bebe told me, 'Come on, mama, stop bothering *[no jodás más]*. Shut up....'" Irma smiles when she remembers what came after that. She went to C&C – "in my slippers, I didn't even comb my hair!" – where she stood outside every store that Bebe entered. She clearly remembers the amount of goods both of them took back home; she also makes a distinction between those who took food products ("stuff they needed") and those who took ("robbed") other objects ("such as TVs, washing machines, freezers, or sneakers"): "We brought a lot of stuff, *but only*," she stresses, "foodstuff.... Not the kind of objects that other people took.... We only took merchandise. Oil, the oil was so expensive then.... We grabbed a great quantity of bottles of oil, and we had yerba, noodles, those boxes of cheap fruit juice.... You don't know how many days we spent drinking that cheap juice!!! Diapers, lots of diapers.... Because my granddaughter was only a month old then, and rice, rice.... We had half a room filled with stuff."

Irma tells me that she shouted from the front door of the store to her son to come out, "because I was a little bit ashamed *[tenía un poco de vergüenza]*, but he screamed back: 'Shut up, *vieja*, don't break my balls.'" Irma's son went several times to C&C, with a cart "he filled up and went back." He took one trip "with a woman who is a Peronist activist, and who had her own car, and who took him to several stores." They were not afraid of the police, Irma said, because there was nobody around. Nobody organized, she said, but she saw some groups breaking the metal gates first; then everybody got in. The merchandise they took out of the stores was left, temporarily, at a relative's house who lived closer than they did to C&C: "We then had to leave some stuff [for this relative] as a sort of payment.... After the *saqueo*, we began to exchange stuff [*el trueque*]. I distributed a lot of goods to my whole family, and I got a lot of cheap things." The night after the episodes was, Irma recollects, "frightening... because they were saying that they were coming to loot us – *iban a saquear a los saqueadores*. I didn't sleep that night; I was very scared because they were saying that people from the barrio 22 de Enero were coming to rob. I electrified the front gate of my house.... But nothing happened, nobody came."

By now, I have conducted and read dozens of interviews with looters, the looted, and bystanders. The facts of Irma's story do not surprise me: I now know that the looting was a joint enterprise (most people went with a relative or a friend, just like Irma); that people found out about the nearby episodes through their neighbors more often than from the TV ("*vecinos* passed by saying that there were lootings... and I went to check them out," as Irma recalls); that there was a "looting vanguard" (those who, as Irma succinctly described, took the initiative and broke the metal gates); that there was a sort of sequence (first taking food products, then other items) in the destruction; that there was some involvement of party activists; that the crowds were quite heterogeneous (many "petty thieves" were present, as both the minister of the interior and dozens of neighbors told me); and that rumors about imminent attacks coming from nearby barrios sent people back home. But something struck me in Irma's tone when I asked her about the store owners who were looted. I've known Irma for years now, and my assertion should not be read as an attempt to pass a moral judgment (a verdict, so to speak) on Irma's behavior but as a sincere interest in her own moral worldview: "Poor people... I mean, the looted [*los saqueados*]... the looters really destroyed them." She looked at me, and then looked away. As if she had never thought about this before, she said: "Well... Yes..." There was a silence. I let the silence linger. She then added: "But those who were looted are not around anymore. They left. They are no longer in Crovara and Cristianía. They sold their stores. One had a heart attack; another one killed himself. But they are no longer there. They weren't even there when the lootings happened."

Many of those looted were, in spite of what Irma said, in their stores while the lootings were going on; they witnessed the destruction and have painful memories of those days. Many of those looted are, further contrary to Irma's remarks, still working in C&C (though some, in both sites, left, bankrupt and unable to reopen after all the damage). Irma's denial of the victims' presence (then and now) is, I presume, a way of dealing with an uncomfortable moral fact: Her room was half-filled with needed goods at someone else's expense, someone as hard-working, someone leading as difficult a life as she was and is. This contradiction is laden with implications, and I need to further explore the looters' moral universe.

Jack, the Looter

Almost two decades ago, sociologist Jack Katz wrote *Seductions of Crime*, an insightful and provocative phenomenological exploration of the moral and sensual attractions of deviant behavior. In substantive terms, the book explores the different experiences of diverse types of crime (from stickups to shoplifting, from murder to membership in an urban gang) asking of each type the same questions: What are the sensual dynamics involved in deviant behaviors? How is crime experienced by criminals? Exactly what is the individual trying to accomplish when she engages in criminal behavior? Drawing on a variety of mostly qualitative sources, the result is a tour de force into the deviants' hearts and minds (and their guts, and their feelings) that shifts attention away from materialistic considerations and into moral, sensual, aesthetic ones in the explanation of crime. In methodological terms, the book enacts "analytic induction" – a way of going about thinking and doing research that Katz first put forward in *Poor People's Lawyers* (1982) and later pursued in other work (1988, 1999) – and shifts attention from background conditions (usually codified in terms of variables that are the preferred focus of most sociologists) to the foreground of deviance – to the seductiveness that crime has for the criminal. This attraction is, Katz argues in what I think is one of the book's most interesting insights, in part a construction of criminals themselves. In other words, the book asks us to move the analytic focus from the causes of crime to the attraction that doing evil conveys to perpetrators.

Existing research on collective violence (e.g., Bourgois 2003; Schneider and Schneider 2003; Armstrong 1998; Kakar 1996) shows that popular conceptions and meanings of violence are contingent on time and place, and that the exercise of damage-making actions sometimes expresses joint notions of pride, respect, and dignity. Collective violence, scholars agree, almost always "makes sense." Anthropologist and historian Anton Blok (2001:9) writes: "The use of physical force, even in its most brutal and enigmatic forms, is rarely 'meaningless' or 'senseless'. On the contrary, it is often honorific – especially under conditions of political insecurity when people 'have to make themselves respected'. The expression 'senseless violence'... is a misnomer, produced by divorcing violence from its context." Collective violence, furthermore, *always* makes some sense from at least one viewpoint – that of the perpetrators.

Taken together, Katz's phenomenological approach to deviant behavior and culturalist perspectives on collective violence leads us to ask similar questions about the lootings: What were looters trying to do? How did looters construct their experiences? What are the dominant, if any, moral and sensual themes in their actions? This last chapter takes up this task.

If anything, the previous pages have situated the episodes in their context – a context of widespread misery, of general uncertainty and anxiety about basic material living conditions, and (most importantly) a more immediate context of opportunity. As mentioned before, analytically the creation of opportunities for looting (an outcome of the actions of brokers, authorities, and cops; an emergent product of the gray zone) and looters' taking advantage of those opportunities are two different processes. The bulk of my argument and evidence concentrates on the first; in what follows, I will focus briefly on the second process by reconstructing participants' experiences.

The first question (What were looters trying to do?) will raise more than one incredulous eyebrow – at least among the readers that saw the events on TV or read about them. Who in his right mind would ask such a foolish question? The looters were trying to get the goods... as many as they could in a limited amount of time. Materialistic considerations abound among looters, true. But if we stick to the details of the events, we see another important dimension. In the process, from the time they got together in front of a market waiting for and/or demanding food, residents-becoming-looters were also justifying their actions in dissimilar but limited, and curiously (given that events occurred in many different locations throughout the country) patterned ways. They did so in their brief statements that were broadcast by the media and by what they said to the authorities that were present – they were even trying to justify their actions to gun-wielding cops. What were they saying? What were their statements trying to accomplish? To foreshadow: in stressing hunger and need, most of the looters (which means most of the looters who cared to talk to the press and to us years later) tried to erect and defend the image of the Righteous Looter – the looter who was, to quote from the *Oxford English Dictionary*, "just, upright, virtuous; guiltless, sinless; conforming to the standard of the divine or the moral law; acting rightly or justly." Within the category of Righteous Looter, there is, however, more than one nuance.

"We want to eat...we are hungry." Hardly surprisingly, that was the dominant theme in the roar of the looting crowd. From greater Buenos Aires to Rosario and Tucumán, in every looting episode, people voiced their desire in terms of a basic need: food. But that was hardly all. That common denominator underlines some other important "reasons why" behind looters' actions. Together with their needs, and even more important than those, looters were defending their right to feed their families.

"I have five kids, and we have no food. We are all unemployed in my family. The only thing we want is bread and milk," said Guillermina, while looting a supermarket in Tucumán (*La Gaceta*, December 20), in a statement that was echoed time and again in many other parts of the country. A woman in Rosario (*El Ciudadano*, December 15) put it this way: "We are hungry, we want food; we want to work. We have big families, we all have four or five kids, and we can't feed them." Together with their children's natural right to food, looters mentioned their unwillingness to loot, even as the looting is taking place – stressing another moral theme in their actions: "We come to ask for food because we don't have anything to feed our kids. We don't want to rob or to loot [*no queremos robar ni saquear*]," said a woman in Tucumán, and a man added: "We are not robbers, we don't want TVs or other valuables. We want food" (*La Gaceta*, December 21). A day after the lootings in Rosario were over,

Liliana articulated her "reasons why" in the following ways. Note how she combines an emphasis on her right to feed her family and a moral theme related to the value of work (as opposed to hustle, meaning in this case, looting):

> I went [to the looting site] to see what was going on, but that day I was sort of angry because I didn't have anything to feed my kids. I was a spectator, because I'd never been to a looting, I never liked that. I always enjoyed earning my money by working, but now things are tough and you have to hustle [*rebuscártelas*] with whatever you have.... That day I was so desperate that I told myself, "Oh, well, if they are looting, why not me?" because desperation leads you to do anything...when the kids are hungry. *I have four kids and three grandkids. I didn't know how to feed them that day. How could I explain to them that there was no food?"* (*El Ciudadano*, December 23, my emphasis)

Standards of right and wrong were also present among many looters when pointing to those responsible for their suffering: authorities and politicians seen as absent, unwilling, or deceptive: "We are dying of hunger because we are all unemployed. And politicians are to be blamed for that. We can't leave our children without food or milk. They are undernourished [*desnutridos*]," said Carmen while she was looting the "Super 24" in Banda del Río Salí, Tucumán (*La Gaceta*, December 20). "We are hungry, where's the mayor?" screamed a woman in the midst of a looting in the Conurbano. "We are going to demand from the big supermarkets what the authorities don't want to give us," a resident of the neighborhood of San Lorenzo in Neuquén told reporters (*Rio Negro On Line*, December 19). "We can't take this anymore," a neighbor of La Palmera in Rosario said. "They promise us boxes of food, and they don't bring enough for everybody. This morning they distributed 120 boxes, but 60 families were left without anything. We spent hours calling them from a pay phone with the few coins we have. They asked us to do something, and then they don't pay attention to us. We blockade the road, and they shoot rubber bullets. What are we, animals?" (*El Ciudadano*, December 19). Another moral antagonism emerged when would-be looters found out about the contents of the boxes that some supermarkets were distributing to avert damage: a youngster in Comodoro Rivadavia put it this way when opening a box, "They are not going to spend Christmas eating this. We don't eat [this kind of] shit" (*Diario Crónica*, Chubut, December 21).

Most of the emphasis then is on the *need* that made them "do it," on themselves as victims of a desperate situation, and on the lootings as the outcome of "no other way out." Nadia, from Rosario, put it this way: "Four months ago they cut the *Planes Trabajar*. Two months ago they stopped giving the bags with food. And yesterday, they closed the soup-kitchen. What are we going to do?" (*El Ciudadano*, December 15). Sometimes, need and the right to feed themselves and their families came with shame. As the woman cited at the beginning of this book said: "I am 30 years old. Can you imagine how ashamed my father is [*la vergüenza de mi papa*] as he watches me doing this?" For a few of those interviewed, there was not so much shame but something thrilling, even exciting, about being able to enter a shop and "take as much stuff as I wanted to," as Pelu told us.

While necessity was a dominant theme in the looters' (re)creation of the looting experience, others mentioned their aspirations (not so much their needs): Good looting came to impersonate their hopes for the future. Delia and her brother (mentioned before) put it this way: "For once, the people had the chance to eat a piece of [gourmet] cheese, a kind of cheese that they'd never tried before. It was the best Christmas we had. We were all happy. We ate a lot, we drank champagne and the best wines." And her brother adds: "You saw smoke coming from everywhere. Everybody was barbecuing. Everybody had new clothes and toys for their children." Paraphrasing Katz, we could say that the lootings were made for Delia and her brother, the cheese gourmet (and for the many others who described to us that opulent Christmas). The looted goods made this, as a youngster in Rio Negro put it, "The best Christmas of my life."

Q: So, were the lootings right or wrong?

BRIAN: The lootings were right...

ZEFERINO: Money was needed...

JONATHAN: And it was Christmas, and there were people who were about to eat some stew, and they wanted to eat a good chicken...

ARIEL: They ate a wonderful barbecue!

JAVIER: Meat, chicken, everything!

ZEFERINO: They ate for Christmas, for New Year, and until Three Wise Men January 6.

(Excerpt from a dialogue we had with "The Guys from Villegas" – a group of youngsters who routinely hang out on one of the corners in the barrio BID)

"Property," Katz (1988:69) tells us, "has boundaries separating insiders, or authorized users, from outsiders, or unauthorized occupants, and these boundaries are often sensed as sacred." Not so at the liminal moment of the lootings. Few regarded *food-property* as something to be protected or valued. In fact, all the participants we interviewed differentiated the looting of food from the stealing of other goods – pretty much along Irma's lines (cited in the field notes at the beginning of the chapter). The lootings had, for participants, a twofold sequence and a twofold crowd: thus, there was a moral binary: good looting and bad looting (defined as stealing). What from the outside looked to be one crowd, doing one (wrong) thing, from the looters' points of view was quite different. Let me cite a few excerpts from dialogues we had with residents of Villegas:

"There was a lot of hunger, need, people were in need [*la gente estaba necesitada*]. But there were also people who stole stuff, like appliances. Those were the crooks who wanted to steal. But those who looted food markets were those in need. There were also people who went to C&C in their trucks. They didn't need anything." (Patricia)

"The lootings happened because there were a lot of people in need. ... I know people who were in very bad shape then, there was no work, nothing. But there were also people who loot because they are evil." (Andrés)

"The lootings might have happened because there was no money to buy anything ... but there were also a lot of crooks. If it were for food, they wouldn't have broken into the furniture store, or into a jewelry store, or into the sneakers store. You can't eat sneakers, or furniture, or the cash register machine." (Leonor)

"Among the looters, there were people who were hungry, truly hungry, and there were thieves." (Adriana)

As I hinted in my field note of July 26, the big absence in participants' testimonies is comments about the looted. Few mentioned owners, managers, and/or employees as lootings' victims. When, for example, I asked Delia about them, about what she thought about the store owners, managers, and employees who suffered the devastation, she replied, "A looting is a looting," implying that that's how things are, that someone has to pay the price in a looting. A few, however, did mention lootings' immediate victims but avoided taking any moral responsibility for their damage-making actions. As Jaquelina, in Las Heras, Mendoza, put it: "Supermarkets throw away the food that they don't need...they all have insurance, so they don't lose anything" (*Los Andes OnLine*, December 17). Liliana, from Rosario, was one of the few who addressed the wrong-headed actions of the looters:

> It was not my intention to ask for food. I think that the supermarket owners are in the same situation as we are. We have to go and break everything for those who are in the government, because they [supermarket owners] are workers as we are, and they struggled a lot to have what they have. It's not fair that we go and destroy their lives [*no es justo que vayamos a cagarle la vida a ellos*]. (*El Ciudadano*, December 23)

There is really not such a thing as a monolithic looter's point of view on the lootings (no single "Jack, the Looter" that encapsulates the rest), on what the lootings meant, but instead there is a series of differing and sometimes contrasting points of view. In all their diversity (from the thrill of stealing and avoiding the police to the shame of being "forced" to do so by circumstances beyond one's control) most of these different points of view share three elements: first, the experience of looting is utilitarian – directly related to the stuff they take. But it also has an additional selectively moral dimension: Looting advocated certain standards of right and wrong while it was oblivious to others. In other words, the looting was a desperate action but also a moral one that sought to uphold a right ("We have to feed our families"), to redress an injustice, and to point blame at those who are perceived as doing wrong without regard for those who paid the real price of the looters' actions (i.e., shopkeepers). Second, looters' experiences are marked by an additional element: Looting was possible, most of our interviewees remarked, because of the opportunity that was created. Once that opportunity was created, looters – moral beings in defense of their right to feed their families – suspended other sorts of moral considerations (those pointing not to their own suffering but to that of their victims). To paraphrase an old proverb, the opportunity made the looter. Third and last, violence, damage-making, and destruction, are rarely mentioned by looters. It is as if from need (to feed their families and themselves) a magic leap is made to the possession of goods: Nothing is broken or damaged in getting them. Violence only becomes an issue when they (the looters) suffer it at the hands of repressive forces, not when the victims are shopkeepers. Violence against property owned by others is erased.

Morality, need, shame, and opportunism emerge then as central themes when looters are asked about the hows of the lootings. When, toward the end of our conversations, we asked them (knowingly violating one of the rules of ethnographic interviews) to tell us why they thought the lootings occurred, we noted more convergence in perspective (a looter's point of view, if you will): All of them mentioned the word "politics" as the root cause of the lootings. And they were not alone in doing so. Interestingly, they agreed with their victims. Both looters and looted see in politics (i.e., in party politics, in the doings and dealings of party leaders and state officials) the main reason why the episodes occurred and when and how they occurred. The next and last section will consider the victims' points of view about these episodes, the points of view and emotions that (although highlighting material losses) are also loaded with moral and political considerations.

Alicia, Barrio BID, July 2005

Since she was one year old, Alicia has lived in barrio BID. She is now 40 and HIV-positive. Her partner died of AIDS a couple of years ago. She has three children –Sofía, who is 17 and addicted to free-base cocaine[1]

---

[1] On the changing patterns of drug consumption among the poor of the Conurbano, see Epele (2005).

(she had just learned she was pregnant when we interviewed her); Daiana, who is 13 and is, according to her mother, smoking pot quite regularly with her friends; and Edgardo, who is 7. Alicia also lives with her mother, who is paralyzed in a wheelchair and can hardly hear anything. Alicia receives a *Plan Jefas y Jefes* (that she got through the local Peronist broker), and her mother has a pension that mostly goes to pay for the medicine she takes. The kids, when they are around, help Alicia by scavenging bottles and newspapers that add an extra $30 to the meager $150 monthly welfare check.

We interviewed her twice, with her children present, and both times we left the house extremely disturbed. After years of conducting ethnography among the poor, I've never seen such a thing: an almost impossible family life that Alicia tries desperately to pull together, but, at the same time, that she destroys with her random violence against the kids (no doubt an expression of her being overwhelmed), against her mother, and against herself (she is an alcoholic). An analysis of her life and all the structural forces conspiring against her is beyond the scope of this book. What follows is an edited version of Alicia's and her daughter Sofía's recollections of the lootings. They summarize important parts of the dynamics and morality of the collective violence that visited C&C during December 2001.

ALICIA: I was watching the news on TV and saw that my neighbors passed by screaming "Alicia, they are looting in Crovara!" And I asked myself, "What shall I do?" She [her daughter] was not here. I picked up a huge yellow bag and went to look for my sister and brother. My sister told me, "No way, I'm a stupid worker [*una gila laburante*]. I won't go even if everybody is going." So I went to see [her brother] Tito. A neighbor of Tito told him: "Come on, let's go..." And they got into his car. But my brother told me: "No, you stay. If I bring something, we'll share. You are useless [*no servís ni para tocar el timbre*]." In my family, they rang the bell before breaking into a house. That's how bad we are at stealing. We might be drunkards, but not thieves. So Tito left me at home. I waited for him here[...] [When they came back] the trunk of the car was filled with stuff, everything for Christmas...mayonnaise, cider, tomato purée...everything. Detergent, bleach...[...] The whole barrio was a mess....Everybody running, here, there. Everybody carrying Adidas sneakers...

sofía: People were carrying home appliances, TV sets, everything! And they were saying that they were stealing food! How come they were taking the TV sets?

alicia: How come they were stealing home appliances?

[. . .]

sofía: Then word started running around that they were coming from other neighborhoods to rob here. . . . The kids closed off the alleyways . . .

alicia: Everybody guarded their own plot. . . .

sofía: They were all lies. . . . The police made it all up. . . .

[. . .]

alicia (REFERRING TO THE STORE OWNERS): Poor guys, because they've worked all their lives, and some *negros de mierda* stole everything. Why? Because they are hungry? And whose fault is that? It's the government's fault because they are not giving the aid they needed. Politicians filled their pockets. And what about the hunger of the poor people? Nobody cares about that. So, people do what they can. When they had the opportunity, they went and stole in order to eat. *Robar para comer!* But, stealing TVs and all that stuff, that's egoism. . . . But stealing noodles, and stuff to eat, that's different.

The Bitter Hereafter

Most Argentines have recollections about the 2001 lootings; even if they were far from the epicenters of violence. Almost every single person I talked to in the country about this project (friends, family, journalists, looters, bystanders, the looted, officials, party members, grassroots leaders, even Argentines who live abroad) remembers Whan Cai So (shown in Figure 8). Whan – or Juan, for locals – was the Korean-born owner of a store in Ciudadela, in the western part of the Conurbano. Whan's store was devastated, and the destruction was broadcast live on TV. What most people I talked to remember, though, is not the destruction but the image of Whan, crying profusely, unable to speak, uttering random words in his broken Spanish. People remember Whan's desperation. They also remember – because it was repeatedly broadcast – the image of a looter, carrying a plastic fully adorned Christmas tree, walking unconcernedly behind Whan while the latter wailed: "*Nada . . . nada . . .*"

Figure 8. Looting at Whan's Store.

There was no ethnic pattern to the looting; the selectivity of the violence was related to the size of markets, police (under)protection, and community and political relations. Some Korean-owned stores were attacked, but I found no evidence of their overrepresentation among the looted or about some (ethnic) intentionality. Whan's story is important not because it illustrates a pattern in the apparently chaotic violence, but because it summarizes the pain that store owners felt at the time (and still feel when remembering those days). Most of them were not physically hurt. Their suffering lies elsewhere. I would not dare to claim that I can read hearts or minds, but Whan's (and most of the shopkeepers we talked to) tears were not solely, not even mainly, about material losses. They were (and, still are) about the arbitrariness of violence. Why them? Why, they ask in their long recollections of the bitter hereafter, should they be paying for (a) the hunger of others and (b) the political dealings "up there"? Let me further elaborate.

Most shopkeepers have trouble putting a figure on the material losses they suffered – those who recall say that they lost between U.S.$30,000 and $60,000 (they vividly bring to mind, however, that their debts were in U.S. dollars and they tripled after devaluation took effect months after the episodes). As I said before, none of our interviewees at both sites were indemnified. Many of them filed paperwork at both municipalities to no avail. As the owner of a looted store in El Cruce told us: "Forget about it. There were all these promises, and then the mayor changed. Someone else came, and nothing happened." Another shopkeeper in C&C captured the state's inattention in this way: "The state did not even give us a tissue so that we could use it to cry about the whole thing."

When talking with us, shopkeepers (owners and employees alike) spent some time in describing the damage their stores suffered and the merchandise they lost – more so when the looted goods were not foodstuff. If it was all about hunger, they asked, how come they looted the clothing store, the sneakers store, the jewelry? "Come on man, you can't eat those things!" we were repeatedly told. As Mario, from C&C, told us:

> "It is as if someone broke into your house.... You feel useless, incapacitated. You ask for help and there's none. You come back to the store and all you find are the bare walls. And you start crying. And you ask yourself: how come they took the shelves? Or the cash register? They said it was hunger [that caused the lootings]: You don't eat the clothes; you don't eat the cash register.... I'll always say that."

As we saw in the previous section, on this, shopkeepers agree with many of the looters we interviewed. For both, looting food products is somehow justified because it's done *por hambre, por necesidad*. On the contrary, sacking nonfood products is defined, by looters and looted alike, as stealing.

The formal interviews and informal conversations we had with shopkeepers were some of the most difficult dialogues we had in the course of fieldwork (although Alicia and a few others competed with these for the disturbing emotions they triggered in us). The facts of the destruction are well known by shopkeepers. They are recounted in a matter-of-fact tone ("This gate was torn apart," "This wall was all damaged," "The windows were all broken," "They took all the stuff... even the toilet bowl," etc.). When their recollections reach the days after the lootings, the tone becomes gloomy, their voices break, and their eyes are filled with tears. That's when they begin to talk about the meanings the events had for them (because that's what they were for them, *events* in the strong sense of life-altering episodes). Images, metaphors, and real stories of sickness and death abound in their testimonies. Below are four samples of what was a common thread among shop owners and their employees at both sites:

> "At that time, I think I had the will to keep going on.... But it *is* [sic] not easy. You are broke, and you are indebted, and you live badly. You live badly. You continually live remembering what happened. It is as if someone is dead, and you keep remembering him. Once you are dead, you are dead. There's no solution. And this is the same. You speak about it, you chat about it with people, and you ask yourself: Why didn't I do something differently? It is as if you are sick and you ask yourself why you didn't seek treatment before. Why didn't I remove all the merchandise from the store before it all happened? I couldn't. It took me by surprise, badly. And they killed you fast, and you died fast. That's it." (Sergio, owner of a looted clothing store in Moreno, my emphasis)
>
> "The owner got really depressed. He got sick... he has cancer now, he is dying." (Mario, employee of a looted food store in Moreno)
>
> "See, it is as if they've killed something that is yours.... They killed my two sons... because they used to give me work; they used to give me money." (Pedro, owner of a looted store in Moreno)
>
> "They left nothing [in the store]. Morally... You see [...] I got depressed, for a long time [I was depressed], because all the sacrifices we put into this, and everything was gone. Because one made a lot of sacrifices to get this." (Roxana, owner of a looted store in C&C)

"Because the problem," said Alberto whose store was destroyed in El Cruce, "is not a material one. I'm not angry because of the material stuff. That stuff comes and goes. But, morally speaking, it's degrading. It's incredible. Do you have any idea how impotent you feel when they are taking the stuff away, and the [police] authorities are right there looking, and they tell you that they have orders not to do anything? That's a shame. Where's the law, where's the State? They do not exist. How come they speak about democracy?" Another shopkeeper puts it this way: "Impotent . . . that's how you feel." This statement that was repeated over and over during the course of our interviews. Impotence, as when someone breaks into your house, someone gets sick for unexplainable reasons, and/or someone dies. In the case of shopkeepers, their impotence is compounded by a sense of being both unprotected (by the police) and attacked (not by looters but by political dealings "up there"). As Mario, from El Cruce told us, "For me, the lootings were all about politics. Those of us at the bottom are always the victims. Those on top are never affected."

Interestingly, their impotence, their quiet crying, their anger about what happened is not directed at the looters as perpetrators of violence (as many a shopkeeper told us, "There's no resentment against them"), but it is intricately related to what most of them perceive as the source of all the violence: state and party politics. State and party politics were, most of them believe, the source of the violence and of their lack of protection. Pascual, whose store in C&C was not looted but who has a keen appreciation of the overall meaning that the episodes had for the looted at both sites, summarizes pages and pages of transcripts:

> "In order to organize this, you have to be really evil. You can have whatever political ideology you want, but you are making damage here, making damage to someone else. Is it really worth it to destroy the store of someone who is struggling hard?"

No store owner or employee was able to precisely describe the "dealings up there," what they call "the political maneuvering." But they are all persuaded that the violence, the destruction, the mayhem, "*todo el desastre*," were the products of "something obscure" as Pascual said during the course of a long meditation about the lootings' hereafter. They all have some intuitive understanding of the gray zone, that obscure and obscured zone where politics, everyday life, and violence meet with sometimes-unpredictable results.

On Morality and Politics

Gladys – quoted at the beginning of this chapter – and many other store owners say they do not want to remember the episodes. But it is hard for them to forget. And when they start talking about their recollections, the past and the present collide. People like Gladys grab the opportunity afforded by the interview to talk about what they think was (and is) right and wrong, what was (and is) fair and unfair, and what authorities should have done during the events, and what they should and should not do (today) about their current daily problems. Irma and many looters and eyewitnesses also used the interviews to articulate their standards of justice and injustice and their views about the (in)actions of government officials. In other words, people like (the looted) Gladys and (the looter) Irma talk, simultaneously, about morality and politics. In all the many conversations we had with victims and perpetrators, moral standards appear intertwined with (state and party) politics. And politics seems to permeate their understandings of the causes of (and possible solutions to) their everyday problems (not only the ones that anteceded the lootings but also those present now). Different from other times and places, these residents do not talk about their suffering by invoking personal merits or failures; their problems do not come from a world inhabited by witches or gods (nor do the solutions come from them). It is politics which, most of the time, is seen as the source of injustice, unfairness, and arbitrariness in everyday life and in more extraordinary circumstances (epitomized in the collective violence suffered by store owners). Politics, however, is experienced as something done elsewhere, an activity in which they are not agents – though, with enough connections, they believe they can avoid politics' worst outcomes. In other words, neither those who perpetrated the violence (and those who witnessed it up close) nor those who endured it see themselves as the source of political power but as the victims.

Countless times during the course of our fieldwork, we heard the expression "It's all politics. What can we do? It's all about politics." When discussing the distribution of welfare in the neighborhood or the kind of food provided by communal soup kitchens, when chatting about police actions during the lootings or about the rising incidence of crime in

148

their neighborhoods, even when talking about their future (individual and collective) prospects, residents in Moreno and La Matanza expressed their views in the language of politics. They were not, however, referring to a joint transformative capacity nor to a collective struggle for resources. They were certainly not referring to specific public policies nor to debates in Congress. "Politics" (as in the expression "it's all about politics"), connotes something profoundly disempowering for them ("What can we do?"). When speaking about politics, they refer to something coming from above, something beyond their control – sometimes they hint at a sort of conspiracy, but most of the time they use the language of politics to talk about how impotent and vulnerable they feel. Their moral universe is infused by politics, and this is the source of the (mostly bad) deeds that they do not fully comprehend and about which they are powerless.

Conclusions

When officials and politicians talk about governability... what do you
think they are talking about? Do you think they refer to their ability to
pass a law in Congress? To have one or two more party members in the
House? No. No way. Listen carefully. They are talking about the capacity
to generate a big mess [*un gran quilombo*] in the Conurbano. That's what
they mean when they say governability.

Interview with Luis D'Elia, July 2005

The December 2001 lootings in Argentina can (and should) serve to
open a broader inquiry into the relational underpinnings of collective
violence. The massive damage visited on people and property during
that December constitutes an extreme event that, as Marcel Mauss (1979
[1916]) asserted a long time ago, is marked by "an excessiveness which
allows us better to perceive the facts than in those places where, although
no less essential, they still remain small-scale and involuted." It is precisely this excessiveness that acts as an invitation to scrutinize the gray
zone where everyday life, routine politics, and collective violence sur-
reptitiously intersect and interact. This book has done so by paying special attention to the role of "third parties" (political brokers and police
agents) who, as the American Sociological Association's report on the
social causes of violence asserts (Levine and Rosich n/d:70), "are often
involved or present during violent encounters; yet, our knowledge of
their role is very limited." The more attention we pay to these third
parties and to their mutual relations, the more blurred the lines that separate everyday life, routine politics, and extraordinary collective violence

appear – a trichotomy, I should add, that remains at the core of breakdown theories of collective behavior (Useem 1998; Snow et al. 1998).

In one of his recent writings, Charles Tilly (2003:40) asserts that throughout the world "specialists in violence figure importantly in the larger-scale versions of collective violence.... [I]n any of their many guises, they often initiate violent political interaction, sometimes cause non-violent political interaction to turn violent, and frequently determine the outcome of political interaction, whether violent or otherwise." And, in a statement that seemed to have been written with the Argentine lootings in mind, Tilly (2003:40, my emphasis) deduces one key implication from the foggy place occupied by violent specialists:

> [A]lthough it will help to start with distinctions among agents of governments, polity members, challengers, and outside political actors, in closer looks at actual . . . episodes we will have to recognize mobile and intermediate actors, political entrepreneurs and violent specialists prominent among them. *No simple distinction between "insurgents" and "forces" of order can possibly capture the complex interactions that generate collective violence.*

The statement succinctly captures my own journey into the lootings: I began, probably naively, with the clear-cut distinctions that figure prominently in political science studies and in collective action scholarship – state agents, political leaders, and victims on one side, perpetrators of violence on the other. The more I looked at what actually happened before and during that violent week, at the interactions between actors who were supposed to be doing one thing but were actually doing another, the more I realized how ill-equipped we are, as students of violent collective action, to deal with a region of the political and social space that is all too important to keep ignoring. The gray zone where boundaries between authorities and looters blur is, I am now certain, an area worth studying if we are to understand and explain not only what happened during that crucial week but also popular politics in general.

As should be clear by now, the episodes under investigation here (and the gray zone in general) are crammed with paradoxes (the *Oxford English Dictionary* defines paradox as "a statement or tenet contrary to received opinion or belief, *esp.* one that is difficult to believe"); I highlighted those that emerged during my research and inspected them in order to move

Conclusions

my description into an explanation (understood as retrodiction) of the looting dynamics. Should the lootings occur in similar form again (let's hope not), the reader should be able to know which actors did what, which relationships were activated, which mechanisms were put into action, and which forms of communication prevailed during and after the episodes. The reader should be better equipped than I was at the beginning of this journey to understand and explain what went on.

This book unearthed, in as detailed form as the available evidence allowed, the concealed dynamic interactions between looters, political brokers, and police forces that shaped the incidence and form of collective violence. It also highlighted the presence of several mechanisms crucial in the creation (and closing) of opportunities to loot (brokerage, legitimation, signaling spirals, broken negotiations). What did we learn from the Argentine case? How useful is this knowledge? In other words, what does this book's in-depth look at one episode of collective violence teach us about other similar cases? Let me tackle the last question first by presenting the reader a (limited) sample of other food lootings in Latin America. I will then propose a way of examining them based on my knowledge of the Argentine case.

Food lootings took place in almost every Latin American country during the past decade.[1] Whether in the context of subsistence crises brought by natural disasters (droughts, flooding, or earthquakes) or in the context of suddenly imposed grievances due to politicoeconomic crises or in the margins of collective protests against neoliberal policies, Latin American countries have witnessed hundreds and sometimes thousands of desperate people attacking food markets and taking away the merchandise (i.e., looting). The 1989 "*caracazo*" or "*sacudón*" is probably one of the best-known cases of massive looting (Lopez Maya 1999). The state of Vargas, in Venezuela, also experienced food lootings during December 1999 right after the flooding that left thousands deprived

---

[1] Modern industrialized nations saw their share of food riots during the past century. As Lynne Taylor (1996:483) remarks: "Food riots occurred in northern France in 1911, in Britain during the winter of 1916–17, in New York City in 1917, in Toronto in both 1924 and 1933, in Barcelona in 1918, in Vichy France in 1942, and in northern France throughout the German occupation."

of the basic means of subsistence (*El Universal*, December 18, 1999). In April 2002, during the attempted coup against President Chavez, Venezuela was also the site of numerous lootings mainly in low-income *barriadas*.

"Here [in the Brazilian northeast] there have always been droughts and lootings," said Bishop Balduino, president of the *Comisión Pastoral de la Tierra*, about the wave of lootings that spread throughout the state of Pernanbuco during April and May 1998. El Niño provoked an intense six-month-long drought in the region and put thousands of poor and hungry people on the verge of death. Emergency food distribution began only after dozens of lootings took place, many of them apparently organized by the Landless Rural Workers Movement (MST) (see Wright and Wolford 2003; *Clarín*, May 14, 1998).[2]

Brazil and Venezuela are hardly alone in witnessing their citizens forcibly seizing food from markets. After the January 1999 earthquake in center-west Colombia left approximately 1,000 dead, hundreds of distressed inhabitants of the city of Armenia invaded and sacked local food stores. Perú also saw its share of lootings: In June 2002, food lootings took place in the context of protests against the privatization of state-owned electrical companies in Arequipa. In May 2003, the roadblocks that were manned in protest against President Toledo's economic policies created food shortages on the northern coast. Desperate residents of Barranca and Huarney looted local, mainly food, markets. Food looting also occurred during the protests against Bolivian President Sanchez de Lozada in both La Paz and El Alto during February 2003 (lootings that involved attacks on the Coca-Cola Company and on Lyonnaise des Eaux, the French company that has provided water to La Paz since 1997). Finally, Uruguay also saw its citizens plunder food stores. At least sixteen of them were ransacked by dozens of residents of low-income barrios in Montevideo that were affected by one of the worst economic crises in years (*Clarín*, August 2, 2002).

What light does my analysis of the lootings of 2001 shed on these other dissimilar cases? The first obvious lesson we can draw from this

---

[2] As we learn from Mike Davis's book (2001), Bishop Balduino was right: Droughts and lootings in the Brazilian northeast go as far back as the late 1800s.

book is that we need to look at these other cases of episodic collective violence closely: We should cautiously dig into multiple primary and secondary sources in order to carefully reconstruct the actual sequences of events and the different points of view of the actors involved. Needless to say, I would be contradicting the basic purpose of this book if I were to make any substantive claim about cases, such as the aforementioned, I only know about from reading the newspapers.

There are, however, analytical claims to be put forward. Analysts interested in riotous Latin America during the past two decades would certainly benefit from looking at *key background conditions* and the way in which they articulate with local conditions. But if the analyst were to adopt this book's approach to collective violence, she should also (a) examine the *relational underpinnings* and *interactive dynamics* of the episodes closely identifying the mechanisms (and their sequence) at work and (b) scrutinize the (possible) *connections between perpetrators of damage and authorities and/or established political actors.*

Nobel Prize economist Joseph Stiglitz recently called the December 2001 events analyzed here "IMF-riots," and scores of analysts in Argentina and abroad made similar comments. While many of the mentioned food riots were certainly associated with the structural adjustment policies of the supranational lending agencies (if anything, cutting relief is an expression of state-retrenchment), an inspection of the networks and actors involved in these episodes will certainly paint a more intricate picture of the processes at work. World-economic pressures interact in complex ways with regional, national, and local politics in that they involve many different modes of practical glocalizations (Tarrow 2005). My analysis suggests that understandings of collective violence improve when analysis of the vernacular articulations of global processes in concrete localities are examined, as opposed to conceptualizing these events using monolithic, all-encompassing labels such as "IMF-riot."

What are the larger implications of this study? In other words, besides the case of the food lootings, what can we learn from the foregoing analysis? As I mentioned in the Introduction, there are substantive as well as analytical implications. Regarding substantive implications, the many examples provided in this book show that the gray zone, dramatized during the lootings, is in point of fact the infrastructure, the foundation of all kinds of politics. It is not a remnant of the past; it is not alien or primitive. On the contrary, it is an enlarging area in democratic Argentina, north and south, to the right of the political spectrum and to the left. In this sense, I agree with grassroots leader D'Elia when he told me that the threat of collective violence (in his words, "the capacity to generate a big mess in the Conurbano") is part and parcel of really existing politics in contemporary Argentina. How else can we understand the interest and vehemence that public officials and leaders still exhibit in talking about the 2001 lootings? The episodes are hardly part of the dim past; they are very present in politicians' and officials' ways of doing and thinking about politics. What brokers and cops are (secretly) capable of doing (and not doing) is vivid in everybody's mind.

We certainly need to consider the immediate political impacts of these violent episodes as well as their larger "reverberations" (Piven and Cloward 1979). What were the concrete responses to the massive insurgency examined in this book? The rioting had concrete effects in terms of the federal government's (almost immediate) placating efforts: In April 2002, the interim government of President Duhalde launched the *Plan Jefas y Jefes*, a state unemployment subsidy of $150 per month (US$50). Covering close to 1.5 million beneficiaries, it is the largest relief program known thus far in the country. Furthermore, the lootings, together with the *cacerolazos*, were crucial in provoking the political crisis that ended the presidency of Fernando De La Rua.

Even more relevant for the larger implications of my analysis are the aftereffects of these extraordinary episodes. D'Elia candidly highlights them by implicitly referring to what Piven and Cloward (1979:26) term "the power of disruption." In our case, this form of power is not posed by "the poor" (as in the movements analyzed in Piven and Cloward's classic book) but by the actors who are capable of tapping into the clandestine connections that define the gray zone.

With the shrinking of the state that characterizes the last three neoliberal decades, the lack of accountability of repressive forces, the sustained strength of clientelist networks, and the consolidation of urban marginality (the "browning" of Argentina, in O'Donnell's terms), the gray zone becomes increasingly relevant in everyday politics. Those who have the capacity to activate the clandestine connections that define the gray zone will be able to use the threat of violence and, eventually, to dislocate institutional life. Although difficult to quantify, the amount of leverage, of political power, that these actors gain by being (cap)able of using what Piven and Cloward term the "threat of disruption" (1979:35) is immense.

In other words, those who can set in motion the synapses of the gray zone will be capable of creating civil disturbance *and* of keeping it at bay. If my analysis is correct, the power of disruption wielded by sectors of the Peronist Party and of the repressive forces is something to be seriously reckoned with. Relationships between state and society in present-day Argentina should take these actors and their power of disruption into account.

What about this book's general analytical implications? Students of Latin American politics should start paying sustained empirical attention to *clandestinity* in the analysis of routine and contentious politics. We need, in the words of the grassroots leader quoted earlier, to learn how to "listen (and to look) carefully." The kind of politics most analysts see and discuss, the "respectable" politics, the "civilized" kind, the sort that takes place in Congress and in the Pink House and that enjoys media attention, depends to a great extent on the gray zone. We, students of politics, should take the ambiguous and obscure zone seriously, making it the empirical focus of sustained research efforts. In her critique of the overly institutional trend in democratic consolidation studies, Deborah Yashar (1999:102, my emphasis) calls for "more conceptually and analytically nuanced studies of democratic politics." That is, "institutional reforms, political norms, and *practices*." If we are going to pay rigorous scholarly attention to the ways in which "democracy is practiced" (Yashar 1999:97), the gray zone should not be excluded from neither serious theoretical nor empirical consideration. Visible state-society relations are undoubtedly important to the quality of democracy in post-transition Latin America (Friedman and Hochstetler 2002), as are hidden and clandestine links between different political actors.

The lootings reveal an area, usually concealed and thus understudied, where everyday life, routine party politics, and collective violence converge. That everyday life and routine politics intersect and feed into each other is hardly news. To take one recent example, Benedict Kerkvliet's

(2005) detailed study of the power of everyday politics in dismantling state-imposed collective farming in northern Vietnam from the 1960s to the 1980s takes up such a task. Routine party politics and collective violence also overlap as in the case of Jamaican posses whose origin lies in party factionalism (Gunst 1995) or in the case of officially sponsored violence against political opponents (Roldán 2002). Rarely has the intersection of these three seemingly discrete spheres of practice been studied together: Arias's (2004; 2006) recent work on the collusion of crime and politics in the daily life of Brazilian *favelas* is, to my knowledge at least, one of the few examples in Latin America.

Without attention to clandestinity, our understanding and explanation of routine and contentious politics is severely flawed. This became evident to my good friend Pedele, a long-term activist for human rights and progressive politics. This (last) anecdote of his (ultimately failed) incursion into electoral politics condenses the pernicious and durable character of the gray zone. Five years ago, Pedele ran for mayor in the primary of a center-left party that was, at the time, seen as representing the "new way of doing politics." On election day, a group of activists working in his campaign in a shantytown found that another group working for an opposing faction was standing on the corner by the school where voting was taking place. Pedele's opponents had a small bag with money in it; they would stop passersby and offer $50 for their votes. Pedele's campaign workers didn't waste any time; they got a gun and assaulted the opponent activists. They then moved to the opposite corner and, with the money recently obtained, they began to buy votes, this time for Pedele (who found out about this episode a month or so later when going over the surprising electoral results in the district where the shantytown is located). When, puzzled, I asked Pedele about the meaning of this episode he, sort of resigned, replied: "That's how things are now, that's how thing are here." Neither Pedele nor I know the true extent of the damage that this kind of practice does to democratic institutions.

APPENDIX

Modeling the Looting Dynamics

Javier Auyero and Timothy Patrick Moran

Based on a thorough reading of three national newspapers with different political leanings – from left to right; *Página12*, *La Nación*, and *Clarín*, and the main local newspapers of the ten provinces where lootings occurred: *El Ciudadano*, *La Voz del Interior*, *La Mañana del Sur*, *Rio Negro*, *Cronica-Chubut*, *La Gaceta*, *El Litoral*, *El Liberal*, *Los Andes*, and *El Sol*, we constructed a dataset with all the reported looting episodes. Since all the lootings took place during one week, we were able to read every single print and on-line edition of the thirteen newspapers for the week under scrutiny, thus providing an exhaustive dataset that avoids the problems related to sampling techniques (Earl et al. 2004:68).[1]

As said before, for the purposes of data collection, a looting episode was defined as the activity of two or more persons either (a) forcibly seizing objects over restraint or resistance or (b) attempting to seize objects but effectively meeting with restraint or resistance. Some groups gathered in front of markets publicly demanding food without attempting to force entrance. We labeled these episodes "claims for food" and considered them to be conceptually different from looting episodes that, whether successful or not, involved violent confrontation. We found and coded 289 riot episodes, representing every looting, attempted looting, or claim for food reported by the Argentine press to have happened the week of December 14–22 (episodes in the federal capital were excluded from our dataset). Of these, 261 were successful lootings or attempted

---

[1] Once the variables were defined, one of the authors coded the content of all reported events to ensure consistent application of coding rules.

lootings that were rebuffed by force (hereafter simply lootings), and 28 were collective claims for food. Each episode was a discrete event, even though they occurred in one continuous riot week. For each episode, we recorded the following information when it was available.

1. *Location of Episode.* Coded at four levels of analysis (province, statistical metropolitan area (SMA, called *aglomerados* in Argentina), city, and neighborhood).

2. *Number of Participants (estimated).* Coded as a four-category ordinal variable (less than 100, between 100 and 400, between 400 and 600, more than 600) based on either the numerical estimate or the descriptive language used by the reporter.

3. *Type of Market Looted.* Partitioned into three categories: (a) foreign-owned chain superstores (known as *hipermercados*) or other nationally, or provincially owned, chain supermarkets; (b) small, locally owned supermarkets or neighborhood grocery stores; (c) nonfood sites such as pharmacies, shoe stores, bicycle shops, or public buildings.

4. *Presence/Absence of Political Party Brokers.* Evidence of the presence of brokers was based on the descriptive language of reporters. Specifically, this variable was coded "yes" when reporters spoke of "*punteros*" or "*dirigentes barriales Peronistas*" (another term for Peronist brokers). When these terms were unspecified or when language was inconclusive, the variable was coded "no."

5. *Presence/Absence of Police.* In Argentina, police forces are either funded by the federal government (*Policía Federal*) or by the provinces (*Policía Provincial*). The federal police operate within the territory of the federal capital and outside of it when crimes are considered under federal jurisdiction. Provincial police operate within the boundaries of each of the twenty-three states. During the lootings, both federal and state police were active at the looting scenes. If either was reported to be present, or if arrests were reported (marking their presence indirectly), this variable was coded "yes." As with brokers, when the presence of police was unspecified or when language was inconclusive, the variable was coded "no."

6. *Additional Variables.* We also recorded information (when provided) on the number of people arrested (17 episodes), injured (22 episodes), and killed (18 episodes), and whether or not any

Modeling the Looting Dynamics

Table 1. *Frequency Distribution of 261 Riot Episodes by Market Type*

Market Type	Presence of Brokers		Presence of Police	
	Yes	No	Yes	No
Large, chain supermarket	13	79	53	39
Column percent	(19.7)	(40.5)	(56.4)	(23.4)
Row percent	(14.1)	(85.9)	(57.6)	(42.4)
Small, local store	53	116	41	128
Column percent	(80.3)	(59.5)	(43.6)	(76.6)
Row percent	(31.4)	(68.6)	(24.3)	(75.7)

Source: Authors' data

distinguishing characteristics of the rioting group were reported. These events were either too infrequent, or the data proved to be much less available, to be included in the final analysis.

Brokers Show Up in Small Markets. Small Markets Do Not Get Police Protection

Table 1 presents the frequency distribution of the reported presence of brokers and police at the looting site by type of market looted. Of the 289 total episodes in the dataset, the type of market looted was not determinable in five of the episodes. Another 23 occurred in nonfood markets such as public buildings that stored food products for state-funded programs, or pharmacies, shoe stores, and the like. To concentrate on a more homogeneous target site, we excluded these episodes, leaving a subsample of 261. Political brokers were reported at 45 (25 percent) of the looting episodes, and police at 94 (36 percent). Interestingly, however, their presence at the two types of markets differed. For brokers, the column percents are most telling. When brokers were present at the looting, the site was usually a small, local store (Category 2) – 80 percent of the time brokers were reported at such sites, as compared to 20 percent at large, chain supermarkets (Category 1). In the absence of brokers, however, the two market types were looted at closer rates. The opposite is true for police, where the row percents are more interesting. In

Table 2. *Maximum Likelihood Coefficients and Odds Ratio Estimates Predicting Type of Market Looted (1 = Large, Chain Supermarkets)*

Independent Variable	Model 1		Model 2		Model 3	
	Log. Coeff.	Odds Ratio	Log. Coeff.	Odds Ratio	Log. Coeff.	Odds Ratio
Broker presence	−1.02**	0.36	−0.59	0.56	−0.46	0.63
(1 = Yes)	(0.34)		(0.36)		(0.42)	
Police presence	–		1.30***	3.68	1.62***	5.03
(1 = Yes)			(0.29)		(0.39)	
Estimated	–		–		0.42	1.52
participant					(0.25)	
count						
Constant	−0.38*		−1.00***		2.05***	
	(.15)		(.21)		(0.56)	
−2 Log likelihood	328.76		307.58		193.54	
Model chi-square	10.01*		31.18***		30.37***	
N	261		261		177	

Notes: * p < .05 ** p < .01 ***p < .001
Numbers in parentheses are standard errors.
Broker presence and Police presence are dummy variables.
Estimated participant count is a four-category ordinal variable.
Source: Authors' data

terms of police presence at looting sites, type of market does not seem to have made much of a difference, but police nonresponse occurred overwhelmingly at small, locally owned stores.

Brokers Are in the Looting Scenes When No Police Forces Are Around. Police Forces Do Not Care for the Size of the Looting Crowds but for the Size of the Markets Under Attack

To more formally assess these differences, Table 2 presents the results of a logistic regression analysis predicting the type of market looted. Market type is a dummy variable where 1 = Category 1 looting site (large, chain supermarket), and 0 = Category 2 looting site (small, local store). Thus, the signs of the coefficients should be interpreted with respect to large, chain supermarkets. As anticipated by the frequency distribution, Model 1 shows the strong, statistically significant effect of broker presence in small, local market looting. Subtracting one from the odds ratio, we see that the odds of broker presence at a looting site are 64 percent lower when the site is a Category 1 chain supermarket.

But the relationship between brokers and looting site is more complex than brokers simply preferring to direct their followers to small, locally owned markets. The presence of police is added in Model 2, bringing two interesting effects. First, the overall fit of the model is much better. Police presence is an even stronger predictor of market type looted – the odds of police presence at a looting site are 268 percent higher when the site is a Category 1, large chain supermarket. Second, the effect of broker presence is substantially reduced to the point of losing statistical significance. The odds of broker presence at a looting site are still lower when the site is a Category 1 chain supermarket, but this effect is no longer statistically significant when controlling for the presence of police. Thus, even though police response is not affected by the presence or absence of brokers, the reverse is not the case. While the frequency distribution and the results of Model 1 show that brokers seem to direct their followers to small, locally owned stores as opposed to large, chain supermarkets, they seem to be doing so largely because the police are not there. When police presence is held constant across the looting episodes, brokers have no reason to prefer one type of market over another. In short, brokers do not prefer smaller markets, rather they prefer safer ones.

To extend the analysis further, Model 3 addresses the relationship between the size of the crowds and the presence of brokers and police. Intuitively one might expect the number of people involved in the lootings to also be an important factor in determining the effects of broker and police presence – brokers should be able to gather more people through organization, and hundreds of people looting a store might warrant more police action than tens of people. Yet, in Model 3, we see that this variable has altogether no effect on either (a) the overall fit of the model or (b) the size of the predictive effects of market type and broker presence. Police were less likely to respond to lootings at small, locally owned stores regardless of whether brokers were present *or the size of the rioting crowd.*

Table 3. *Frequency Distributions of Police and Broker Presence by Market Type*

	All Incidents ($n = 261$)	
	Presence of Brokers	
Presence of Police	Yes	No
Yes	7	87
	(10.6)	(44.6)
No	59	108
	(89.4)	(55.4)

Chi-square $= 24.75$***

	Large, Chain Supermarkets ($n = 92$)	
	Presence of Brokers	
Presence of Police	Yes	No
Yes	7	46
	(58.9)	(58.2)
No	6	33
	(46.2)	(41.8)

Chi-square $= 0.08$

	Small, Local Markets ($n = 169$)	
	Presence of Brokers	
Presence of Police	Yes	No
Yes	0	41
	(0.0)	(35.3)
No	53	75
	(100.0)	(64.7)

Chi-square $= 25.73$***
Notes: *** $p < .001$
Numbers in parentheses are column percents.
Source: Authors' data

In our dataset the presence of brokers was reported in only 25 percent of the episodes, yet in the 128 episodes for which there exists detailed reporting, 52 percent reported broker presence, suggesting that their presence may be an even greater factor than uncovered here.

Modeling the Looting Dynamics

Evaluating Model 2 for each of the four combinations hints at a more specific understanding of broker and police presence. Based on the model, the expected probability of small, local markets being the looted site is lowest when police are present and brokers are not (.42) and highest when brokers are present and police are not (.83) – a difference of .41. The difference in expected probabilities when brokers and police are both present (.57) and are both absent (.73) is only .16.

These findings are confirmed by a more disaggregated look at the frequency distribution from Table 1 (Table 3). First, the relationship between police presence and broker presence over all 261 episodes leads one to conclude that this relationship is statistically significant (chi-square is 24.75), and that even though the absence of brokers leads to a roughly equal chance of police presence, the presence of brokers almost always is associated with no police (almost 90 percent of the time). But looking at the next two cross-tabs, we see how the broker and police presence connection operates *through* the type of market looted, and more specifically whether or not the looting site is a small, local market. When the site is a big, chain market, there is a higher likelihood of police presence than not, but there is little broker involvement in these episodes, and the chi-square value (0.08) suggests that the episodes are more or less randomly distributed across the four cells. But when the site is a small, local market, we see much more broker activity and a much lower likelihood of police presence. In every episode occurring in these markets, there was never a riot in which brokers and police were both present – in all 53 episodes in which brokers were involved, police were not.

Bibliography

Alarcón, Cristian. 2003. *Cuando me muera quiero que me toquen cumbia. Vidas de pibes chorros*. Buenos Aires: Norma.

Alsina, Griselda and Andrea Catenazzi. 2002. *Diagnóstico preliminar ambiental de Moreno*. Buenos Aires: Universidad de General Sarmiento.

Alford, Robert. 1998. *The Craft of Inquiry*. Oxford: Oxford University Press.

Amin, Shahid. 1995. *Event, Metaphor, Memory. Chauri-Chaura 1922–1992*. Berkeley: University of California Press.

Amato, Alberto. 2002. "La Trama Política de los Saqueos." *Clarín Digital*, December 19.

Arias, Desmond. 2006. "Trouble en Route. . . ." *Qualitative Sociology* 29(4):1–26.

———. 2004. "Faith in Our Neighbors: Networks and Social Order in Three Brazilian Favelas." *Latin American Politics and Society* 46(1):1–38.

———. 2003. "The Infrastructure of Criminal Governance: Illegal Networks and Public Order in Rio de Janeiro." Paper Presented at the 2003 Meeting of the Latin American Studies, Dallas, March 27–29.

Armstrong, Gary. 1998. *Football Hooligans: Knowing the Score*. Oxford: Berg.

Aronskind, Ricardo. 2001. *¿Más Cerca o Ms Lejos del Desarrollo? Tranformaciones Económicas en los '90*. Buenos Aires: Centro Rojas.

Ashforth, Adam. 2005. *Witchcraft, Violence, and Democracy in South Africa*. Chicago: University of Chicago Press.

Auyero, Javier. 2006. "Space and Place as Sites and Objects of Politics." pp. 230–45 in *The Oxford Handbook of Contextual Political Analysis*, edited by Robert Goodin and Charles Tilly. Oxford: Oxford University Press.

———. 2003. *Contentious Lives*. Durham, North Carolina: Duke University Press.

———. 2002. *La Protesta: Retratos de la Beligerancia Popular en la Democrática*. Buenos Aires: Libros del Rojas.

———. 2001. *Poor People's Politics*. Durham, North Carolina: Duke University Press.

———. 2000. "The Hypershantytown. Ethnographic Portraits of Neo-liberal Violence(s)." *Ethnography* 1(1):93–116.

Auyero, Javier and Timothy Moran. 2007. "The Dynamics of Collective Violence: Dissecting Food Riots in Contemporary Argentina." Forthcoming in *Social Forces*.

Aveni, Adrian. 1977. "The Not-So-Lonely Crowd: Friendship Groups in Collective Behavior." *Sociometry* 40(1):96–9.

Baldassare, Mark. 1994. *The Los Angeles Riots: Lessons for the Urban Future*. Boulder, Colorado: Westview.

Barbeito, Alberto and Ruben LoVuolo. 1992. *La Modernizacion Excluyente*. Buenos Aires: Losada.

Beccaria, Luis and Nestor Lopez. 1996. "Notas sobre el comportamiento del mercado de trabajo urbano." Pp. 17–46 in *Sin Trabajo. Las características del desempleo y sus efectos en la sociedad argentina*, edited by Luis Beccaria and Nestor Lopez. Buenos Aires: Losada.

Bergesen, Albert and Max Herman. 1998. "Immigration, Race, and Riot: The 1992 Los Angeles Uprising." *American Sociological Review* 63(1):39–54.

Bessinger, Mark. 1998. "National Violence and the State." *Comparative Politics* 30:401–22.

Betancourt, Darío and Martha Luz García. 1994. *Contrabandistas, Marimberos y Mafiosos. Historia social de la mafia colombiana (1965–1992)*. Bogotá: T/M Editores.

Binder, Alberto. 2004. *Policías y Ladrones. La Inseguridad en Cuestión*. Buenos Aires: Capital Intelectual.

Blok, Anton. 2001. *Honor and Violence*. Oxford: Blackwell.

Bohstedt, John. 1983. *Riots and Community Politics in England and Wales 1790–1810*. Cambridge, Massachusetts: Harvard University Press.

Bonasso, Miguel. 2002. *El Palacio y la Calle*. Buenos Aires: Planeta.

Bourdieu, Pierre. 1997. *Pascalian Meditations*. Stanford, California: Stanford University Press.

2001. *Masculine Domination*. Stanford, California: Stanford University Press.

Bourdieu, Pierre, Jean-Claude Chamboderon, and Jean-Claude Passeron. 1991. *The Craft of Sociology*. Berlin: de Gruyter.

Bourdieu, Pierre and Loïc Wacquant. 1992. *An Invitation to Reflexive Sociology*. Chicago: University of Chicago Press.

Bourgois, Philippe. 2001. "The Power of Violence in War and Peace." *Ethnography* 2(1):5–34.

2003. *In Search of Respect: Selling Crack in El Barrio*. Cambridge: Cambridge University Press.

Forthcoming. *Righteous Dopefiend*. Berkeley: University of California Press.

Bouton, Cynthia. 1993. *The Flour War. Gender, Class, and Community in Late Ancien Régime French Society*. University Park: Pennsylvania State University Press.

Brass, Paul, editor. 1996. *Riots and Pogroms*. New York: New York University Press.

1997. *Theft of an Idol*. Princeton, New Jersey: Princeton University Press.

Bibliography

Braun, Herbert. 1980. The Assassination of Gaitán: Public Life and Urban Violence in Colombia. Madison: The University of Wisconsin Press.

Broadbent, Jeffrey. 2003. "Movement in Context: Thick Networks and Japanese Environmental Protest." Pp. 204–29 in *Social Movements and Networks: Relational Approaches to Collective Action*, edited by Mario Diani and Doug McAdam. New York: Oxford University Press.

Brockett, Charles. 2005. *Political Movements and Violence in Central America*. Cambridge: Cambridge University Press.

Brusco, Valeria, Marcelo Nazareno, and Susan Stokes. 2004. "Vote Buying in Argentina." *Latin American Research Review* 39(2):66–88.

Burawoy, Michael. 1998. "The Extended Case Method." *Sociological Theory* 16: 4–33.

——— 2003. "Revisits: An Outline of a Theory of Reflexive Ethnography." *American Sociological Review* 68(5):645–79.

Cafassi, Emilio. 2002. *Olla a Presión. Cacerolazos, Piquetes y Asambleas, sobre Fuego Argentino*. Buenos Aires: Libros del Rojas.

Calvo, Ernesto and Maria Victoria Murillo. 2004. "Who Delivers? Partisan Clients in the Argentine Electoral Market." *American Journal of Political Science* 48(4):742–57.

Camarasa, Jorge. 2002. *Días de Furia*. Buenos Aires: Sudamericana.

Caplan, Nathan. 1970. "The New Ghetto Man: A Review of Recent Empirical Studies." *Journal of Social Issues* 26(Winter):59–73.

Caplan, Nathan and Jeffrey Paige. 1968. "Survey of Detroit and Newark Riot Participants." pp. 127–37 in *Report of the National Advisor Commission on Civil Disorders*. New York: Bantam Books.

Cardoso, Ruth. 1992. "Popular Movements in the Context of Consolidation of Democracy." Pp. 291–302 in *The Making of Social Movements in Latin America*, edited by Arturo Escobar and Sonia Alvarez. Boulder, Colorado: Westview Press.

Carlos, Manuel and Bo Anderson. 1991. "Political Brokerage and Network Politics in Mexico: The Case of a Dominance System." Pp. 169–87 in *Networks, Exchange and Coercion: The Elementary Theory and Its Applications*, edited by David Willer and Bo Anderson. New York: Elsevier.

CELS (Centro de Estudios Legales y Sociales). 2003. *Plan Jefes y Jefas. ¿Derecho Social o Beneficio sin Derechos?* Buenos Aires: Centro de Estudios Legales y Sociales.

——— 2002. *La Protesta Social en Argentina durante Diciembre de 2001*. Buenos Aires: Centro de Estudios Legales y Sociales.

Cerrutti, Marcela and Alejandro Grimson. 2004. "Buenos Aires, Neoliberalismo y Después. Cambios Socioeconómicos y Respuestas Populares." Princeton University, CMD Working Paper #04–04d.

Cesari, Jocelyne. 2006. "Ethnicity, Islam, and les Banlieues: Confusing the Issues." *www.ssrc.org*, accessed May 6, 2006.

Colectivo Situaciones. 2002. *19 y 20 Apuntes para el Nuevo Protagonismo Social*. Buenos Aires: Ediciones de Mano en Mano.

Comaroff, John and Jean Comaroff. 1992. *Ethnography and the Historical Imagination*. Boulder, Colorado: Westview Press.

Conniff, Michael L. 1981. *Urban Politics in Brazil: The Rise of Populism 1925–1945*. Pittsburg: University of Pittsburgh Press.

Cornelius, Wayne. 1969. "Urbanization as an Agent in Latin American Instability: The Case of Mexico." *American Political Science Review* 63:833–57.

Cutter, Susan. 2006. "The Geography of Social Vulnerability: Race, Class, and Catastrophe." *www.ssrc.org*, accessed March 16, 2006.

Danzger, M. H. 1975. "Validating Conflict Data." *American Sociological Review* 40:570–84.

Das, Veena, editor. 1990. *Mirrors of Violence: Communities, Riots, and Survivors in South Asia* Oxford: Oxford University Press.

Davenport, Christian, editor. 2000. *Paths to State Repression*. New York: Rowman & Littlefield Publishers.

Hank Johnston, and Carol Mueller, editors. 2005. *Repression and Mobilization*. Minneapolis: University of Minnesota Press.

Davis, Mike. 2001. *Late Victorian Holocausts*. New York: Verso.

and Anthony Fontenot. 2005. "25 Questions About the Murder of New Orleans." *The Nation*, September 30, accessed May 9, 2006.

Davis, Natalie. 1973. "The Rites of Violence: Religious Riot in Sixteenth-Century France." *Past and Present* 59(May):51–91.

Della Porta, Donatella. 1996. "Social Movements and the State: Thoughts of the Policing of Protest." Pp. 62–92 in *Comparative Perspectives on Social Movements*, edited by Doug McAdam, John D. McCarthy, and Mayer N. Zald. Cambridge: Cambridge University Press.

1995. *Political Movements, Political Violence, and the State*. New York: Cambridge University Press.

Diani, Mario and Doug McAdam, editors. 2003. *Social Movements and Networks: Relational Approaches to Collective Action*. New York: Oxford University Press.

Di Natale, Martín. 2005. *El Festival de la Pobreza*. Buenos Aires: La Crujía.

Dinerstein, Ana. 2001. "El Poder de lo Irrealizado. El corte de ruta en Argentina y el potencial subversivo de la mundialización." *OSAL*, Septiembre.

Dohan, Daniel. 2003. *The Price of Poverty: Money, Work, and Culture in the Mexican-American Barrio*. Berkeley: University of California Press.

DuBois, Lindsay. 2002. "The Looters are Coming! The Looters are Coming!: Moral Panic and the Argentine Crisis." Paper presented as part of American Anthropological Association Annual Meeting, New Orleans, November 20.

Earl, Jennifer, Andrew Martin, John D. McCarthy, and Sarah A. Soule. 2004. "The Use of Newspaper Data in the Study of Collective Action." *Annual Review of Sociology* 30:65–80.

Earl, Jennifer, Sarah A. Soule, and John McCarthy. 2003. "Protest under Fire? Explaining the Policing of Protest." *American Journal of Sociology* 68:581–606.

Bibliography

Edin, Kathryn and Laura Lein. 1997. *Making Ends Meet: How Single Mothers Survive Welfare and Low-Wage Work.* New York: Russell Sage Foundation.

Ehrenreich, Barbara. 2002. *Nickel and Dimed: On (Not) Getting by in America.* New York: Owl Books.

El Liberal. 2001. *Informe Especial: Los Cimientos del Poder. www.elliberal.com.ar,* accessed February 2, 2003.

Eliasoph, Nina. 1998. *Avoiding Politics: How Americans Produce Apathy in Everyday Life.* Cambridge: Cambridge University Press.

Elison, Graham and Greg Martin. 2000. "Policing, Collective Action, and Social Movement Theory: The Case of the Northern Ireland Civil Rights Campaign." *British Journal of Sociology* 51(4):681–99.

Epele, María. 2005. "Cambios en las Prácticas de Uso de Cocaína: Neoliberalismo, VIH-SIDA y Muerte en el Sur del Gran Buenos Aires." *Apuntes de Investigación* 10:63–85.

Epstein, Edward. 2003. "The Piquetero Movement of Greater Buenos Aires: Working Class Protest During the Current Argentine Crisis." *Canadian Journal of Latin American and Caribbean Studies* 28(55–6):11–36.

Erickson, Bonnie. 1996. "The Structure of Ignorance." Keynote Address, Sunbelt XVI: International Sunbelt Social Network Conference, Charleston, South Carolina, February 22.

Fantasia, Rick. 1988. *Cultures of Solidarity: Consciousness, Action, and Contemporary American Workers.* Berkeley: University of California Press.

Farmer, Paul. 2004. "An Anthropology of Structural Violence." *Current Anthropology* 45(3):305–17.

Feagin, Joe and Harlan Hahn. 1973. *Ghetto Revolts: The Politics of Violence in American Cities.* New York: Macmillan.

Fradkin, Raúl. 2002. *Cosecharás tu Siembra.* Buenos Aires: Prometeo Libros.

Franzosi, Roberto. 1987. "The Press as a Source of Sociohistorical Data." *Historical Methods* 20:5–16.

Friedman, Elisabeth Jay and Kathryn Hochstetler. 2002. "Assessing the Third Transition in Latin American Democratization: Representational Regimes and Civil Society in Argentina and Brazil." *Comparative Politics* 35(1):21–42.

Fussell, Elizabeth. 2006. "Leaving New Orleans: Social Stratification, Networks, and Hurricane Evacuation." *www.ssrc.org,* accessed March 16, 2006.

Gagnon, V. P., Jr. 1994. "Ethnic Nationalism and International Conflict: The Case of Serbia." *International Security* 19:130–66.

Gamson, William A. [1975] 1990. *The Strategy of Social Protest.* Reprint, Homewood, Illinois: Dorsey.

Gay, Robert. 2005. *Lucia: Testimonies of a Brazilian Drug Dealer's Woman.* Philadelphia: Temple University Press.

1994. *Popular Organization and Democracy in Rio de Janeiro: A Tale of Two Favelas.* Philadelphia: Temple University Press.

1990. Community Organization and Clientelist Politics in Contemporary Brazil: A Case Study from Suburban Rio de Janeiro. *International Journal of Urban and Regional Research* 14(4):648–65.

171

Giarraca, Norma, editor. 2001. *La Protesta Social en la Argentina*. Buenos Aires: Alianza.

Gibson, Edward and Ernesto Calvo. 2000. "Federalism and Low-Maintenance Constituencies: Territorial Dimensions of Economic Reform in Argentina." *Studies in Comparative International Development* 35(3):32–55.

Goldberg, Jonathan. 2003a. "Campaign Conscripts: How to Fill a Stadium with Argentina's Poor (and Other Ways to Win the Presidency)." *The American Prospect* (April), On-line Edition, accessed August 23, 2003.

2003b. "Client Privilege." *The American Prospect* (April), On-line Edition, accessed August 23, 2003.

2003c. "Go Between." *The American Prospect* (April), On-line Edition, accessed August 23, 2003.

Goldstein, Donna. 2003. *Laughter Out of Place: Race, Class, and Sexuality in a Rio Shantytown*. Berkeley: University of California Press.

Goldstone, Jack. 2003. "Introduction: Bridging Institutionalized and Noninstitutionalized Politics." Pp. 1–24 in *States, Parties, and Social Movements*, edited by Jack Goldstone. New York: Cambridge University Press.

Goode, Erich. 1992. *Collective Behaviour*. New York: Harcourt Brace Jovanovich.

Gooding-Williams, Robert. 1993. *Reading Rodney King: Reading Urban Uprising*. New York: Routledge.

Gould, Roger. 1995. *Insurgent Identities: Class, Community, and Protest from 1848 to the Commune*. Chicago: University of Chicago Press.

Gould, Roger and Roberto Fernandez. 1989. "Structures of Mediation: A Formal Approach to Brokerage in Transaction Networks." *Sociological Methodology* 1990:89–126.

Grimson, Alejandro et al. 2004. "La vida organizacional en zonas populares de Buenos Aires," The Center for Migration and Development, Working Series Paper, Princeton University, CMD Working Paper.

Guagnini, Lucas. 2003. "Barrabravas en el Estado: La Fuerza de Choque de la Política." *Clarín Digital, Suplemento Zona*, October 19. Accessed January 1, 2006.

Guardian (Manchester). 2006. "France Braced for 12th Night of Riots." November 7. *www.guardian.co.uk*, accessed May 4, 2006.

2006. "America's Ordeal." September 4. *www.guardian.co.uk*, accessed May 3, 2006.

2006. "Katrina's Wrath." September 1a. *www.guardian.co.uk*, accessed May 3, 2006.

2006. "It's Like a War Zone Here: There Was Shooting and Looting." September 1b. *www.guardian.co.uk*, accessed May 3, 2006.

Gunst, Laurie. 1995. *Born Fi' Dead: A Journey Through the Yardie Posse Underworld*. New York: Canongate Books.

Gurr, Ted. 1970. *Why Men Rebel*. Princeton, New Jersey: Princeton University Press.

Guterbock, Thomas. 1980. *Machine Politics in Transition: Party and Community in Chicago*. Chicago: University of Chicago Press.

Bibliography

Hathazy, Paul. 2004. "Cosmologías del Orden: Disciplina y Sacrificio en los Agentes Antidisturbios." Unpublished Manuscript. University of California, Berkeley.

Hibbs, Douglas A. 1973. *Mass Political Violence*. New York: John Wiley and Sons.

Hirsch, Eric L. 1990. "Sacrifice for the Cause: Group Processes, Recruitment, and Commitment in a Student Social Movement." *American Sociological Review* 55:243–54.

Indec (Instituto Nacional de Estadísticas y Censos). 2003. *Encuesta Permanente de Hogares*. Buenos Aires: Indec.

Iñigo Carrera, Nicolás. 1999. "Fisonomia de las Huelgas Generales de la Década de 1990." *PIMSA* 1999:155–73.

Isla, Alejandro and Daniel Miguez, editors. 2003. *Heridas Urbanas. Violencia Delictiva y Transformaciones Sociales en los Noventa*. Buenos Aires: Editorial de las Ciencias.

Jackson, Stephen. 2006. "Un/natural Disasters, Here and There." *www.ssrc.org*, accessed March 16, 2006.

Jenkins, Craig. 1983. "Resource Mobilization Theory," *Annual Review of Sociology* 9:527–53.

Joseph, Gilbert M. 1990. "On the Trail of Latin American Bandits: A Reexamination of Peasant Resistance." *Latin American Research Review* 25(3): 7–53.

Kakar, Sudhir. 1996. *The Colors of Violence: Cultural Identities, Religion, and Conflict*. Chicago: University of Chicago Press.

Kastoriano, Riva. 2006. "Territories of Identities in France." *www.ssrc.org*, accessed May 6, 2006.

Katz, Jack. 2002. "From How to Why: On Luminous Description and Causal Inference in Ethnography (Part II)." *Ethnography* 3(1):73–90.

———. 2001. "From How to Why: On Luminous Description and Causal Inference in Ethnography (Part I)." *Ethnography* 2(4):443–73.

———. 1999. *How Emotions Work*. Chicago: Chicago University Press.

———. 1988. *Seductions of Crime*. New York: Basic Books.

———. 1982. *Poor People's Lawyers*. New Brunswick, New Jersey: Rutgers University Press.

Katzenelson, Ira. 1981. *City Trenches: Urban Politics and the Patterning of Class in the United States*. Chicago: University of Chicago Press.

Kerkvliet, Benedict J. Tria. 2005. *The Power of Everyday Politics: How Vietnamese Peasants Transformed National Policy*. Ithaca, New York: Cornell University Press.

Killian, Lewis. 1980. "Theory of Collective Behaviour: The Mainstream Revisited." Pp. 275–89 in *Sociological Theory and Research: A Critical Appraisal*, edited by Hubert Blalock. New York: Free Press.

Kirschke, Linda. 2000. "Informal Repression, Zero-sum Politics and Late Third Wave Transitions." *Journal of Modern African Studies* 38(3):383–403.

Klachko, Paula. Cutral Co y Plaza Huincul. 1999. "El Primer Corte de Ruta." *PIMSA* 1999:121–54.

Klipphan, Andres. 2004. *Asuntos Internos. Las Mafias Policiales Contadas desde Dentro*. Buenos Aires: Aguilar.

Knoke, David. 1990. *Political Networks*. Cambridge: Cambridge University Press.

Kohan, Aníbal. 2002. *A las Calles! Una Historia de los Movimientos Piqueteros y Caceroleros de los '90 al 2002*. Buenos Aires: Ediciones Colihue.

Kollmann, Raúl. 2005. "Seis Claves de lo que Pasó en Córdoba." *Página12Digital* February 13, accessed March 14, 2006.

———. 2005. "Las Seis Preguntas Clave." *Pagina12Digital* April 13, accessed March 14, 2006.

Koopmans, Ruud and Dieter Rucht. 2002. "Protest Event Analysis." Pp. 231–59 in *Methods of Social Movement Research*, edited by Bert Klandermans and Susan Staggenborg. Minneapolis: University of Minnesota Press.

———. 1999. "Protest Event Analysis –Where to Now?" *Mobilization* 4:123–30.

Kornblum, William. 1974. *Blue Collar Community*. Chicago: University of Chicago Press.

Kriesi, Hanspeter, R. Koopmans, J. W. Dyvendak, and M. Giugni. 1995. *New Social Movements in Western Europe*. Minneapolis: University of Minnesota Press.

Laufer, Rubén and Claudio Spiguel. 1999. "Las 'Puebladas' Argentinas a partir del 'Santiagueñazo' de 1993. Tradición Histórica y Nuevas Formas de Lucha." Pp. 15–44 in *Lucha Popular, Democracia, Neoliberalismo: Protesta Popular en América Latina en los Años del Ajuste*, edited by Margarita López Maya. Venezuela: Nueva Sociedad.

Leeds, Elizabeth. 1996. "Cocaine and Parallel Polities in the Brazilian Urban Periphery: Constraints on Local-Level Democratization." *Latin American Research Review* 31(3):47–83.

Levi, Primo. 1988. *The Drowned and the Saved*. New York: Summit Books.

Levine, Felice and Katherine Rosich. n/d. Social Causes of Violence: Crafting a Science Agenda. American Sociological Association, on-line document at *www.asanet.org*, accessed January 30, 2003.

Levitsky, Steve. 2003. *Transforming Labor-Based Parties in Latin America: Argentine Peronism in Comparative Perspective*. New York: Cambridge University Press.

Levitsky, Steve and María Victoria Murillo, editors. 2006. *Argentine Democracy: The Politics of Institutional Weakness*. University Park: Pennsylvania State University Press.

Lewkowics, Ignacio. 2002. *Sucesos Argentinos*. Buenos Aires: Paidos.

Lieberson, Stanley and Arnold Silverman. 1965. "The Precipitants and Underlying Conditions of Race Riots." *American Sociological Review* 30(6):887–98.

Lofland, John. 1981. "Collective Behaviour: The Elementary Forms." Pp. 411–46 in *Social Psychology: Sociological Perspectives*, edited by Morris Rosenberg and Ralph H. Turner. New York: Basic Books.

Lomnitz, Larissa. 1975. *Cómo sobreviven los marginados*. Ciudad de Mexico: Siglo XXI.

Bibliography

Lopez Echagüe, Hernán. 1996. *El Otro*. Buenos Aires: Planeta.

Lopez Maya, Margarita, editor. 1999. *Lucha Popular, Democracia, Neoliberalismo: Protesta Popular en América Latina en los Años del Ajuste*. Venezuela: Nueva Sociedad.

MacFarquhar, Larissa. 2003. "The Strongman: Where Is Hindu-Nationalist Violence Leading?" *The New Yorker*, May 26:50–7.

Mallamaci, Karina. 2003. "Estudio sobre políticas educativas compensatorias. Formulación e implementación en escuelas básicas de un municipio del conurbano bonaerense." M.A. Thesis. Flacso, Buenos Aires.

Marín, Manuela. 2003. "Empowerment or Dependence? Poverty Alleviation in Greater Buenos Aires." Unpublished Manuscript. Institute of Latin American Studies, London. MSC in Globalization and Latin American Development.

Markoff, John. 1996. *The Abolition of Feudalism: Peasants, Lords, and Legislators in the French Revolution*. University Park: Pennsylvania State University Press.

Martínez, Tomás. 2002. *Episodios Argentinos*. Buenos Aires: Aguilar.

Massey, Doreen. 1984. "Introduction: Geography Matters." Pp. 1–11 in *Geography Matters!*, edited by Doreen Massey and John Allen. Cambridge: Cambridge University Press.

Mauss, Marcel (in collaboration with Henri Beuchat). 1979 [1916]. *Seasonal Variations of the Eskimo: A Study in Social Morphology*. London and Boston: Routledge and Kegan Paul.

McAdam, Doug. 2003. "Beyond Structural Analysis: Toward a More Dynamic Understanding of Social Movements." pp. 281–98 in *Social Movements and Networks: Relational Approaches to Collective Action*, edited by Mario Diani and Doug McAdam. New York: Oxford University Press.

1988. *Freedom Summer*. New York: Oxford University Press.

1982. *Political Process and the Development of Black Insurgency, 1930–1970*. Chicago: University of Chicago Press.

McAdam, Doug and Dieter Ruch. 1993. "The Cross-National Diffusion of Movement Ideas." *The Annals of the American Academy of Political and Social Science* 528:56–74.

McAdam, Doug, Sidney Tarrow, and Charles Tilly. 2001. *Dynamics of Contention*. New York: Cambridge University Press.

McCarthy, John and Mayer Zald. 1977. "Resource Mobilization and Social Movements." *American Journal of Sociology* 82:1212–41.

1971. *The Trend of Social Movements in America*. Morristown, New Jersey: General Learning Press.

McPhail, Clark. 1992. *Acting Together: The Organization of Crowds*. New York: Aldine de Gruyter.

1991. *The Myth of the Madding Crowd*. New York: Aldine de Gruyter.

1971. "Civil Disorder Participation: A Critical Examination of Recent Research." *American Sociological Review* 36(December):1058–73.

McPhail, Clark and John McCarthy. 2005. "Protest Mobilization, Protest Repression, and Their Interaction." Pp. 3–32 in *Repression and Mobilization*, edited by Christian Davenport, Hank Johnston, and Carol Mueller. Minneapolis: University of Minnesota Press.

McPhail, Clark and Ronald Wohlstein. 1983. "Individual and Collective Behaviors within Gatherings, Demonstrations, and Riots." *Annual Review of Sociology* 9:579–600.

Merton, Robert K. 1949. *Social Theory and Social Structure*. Glencoe, Illinois: Free Press.

Minujin, Alberto and Gabriel Kessler. 1995. *La Nueva Pobreza en la Argentina*. Buenos Aires: Planeta.

Mische, Ann. 2003. "Cross-talk in Movements: Reconceiving the Culture-Network Link." Pp. 258–80 in *Social Movements and Networks: Relational Approaches to Collective Action*, edited by Mario Diani and Doug McAdam. New York: Oxford University Press.

Moinat, Sheryl, Walter Raine, Stephen Burbeck, and Keith Davison. 1972. "Black Ghetto Residents as Rioters." *Journal of Social Issues* 28:45–62.

Mueller, Carol. 1997. "International Press Coverage of Eastern German Protest Events." *American Sociological Review* 62:820–32.

Myers, Daniel. 1997. "Racial Rioting in the 1960s." *American Sociological Review* 62:94–112.

and Beth Schaefer Caniglia. 2004. "All the Rioting That's Fit to Print: Selection Effects in National Newspaper Coverage of Civil Disorders, 1968–1969." *American Sociological Review* 69(August):519–43.

Neufeld, María Rosa and María Cristina Cravino. 2003. "Entre la Hiperinflación y la devaluación: 'saqueos' y ollas populares en la memoria y trama organizativa de los sectores populares del Gran Buenos Aires (1989–2001)." Unpublished Manuscript. Universidad Nacional de General Sarmiento.

New York Times. 2005. "Hurricane Katrina: New Orleans; Life-or-Death Words of the Day in a Battered City: 'I Had to Get Out'." August 31. *www.nytimes.com*, accessed May 4, 2006.

2005. "Hurricane Katrina: The Overview; Bush Sees Long Recovery for New Orleans; 30,000 Troops in Largest U.S. Relief Report." September 1. *www.nytimes.com*, accessed May 4, 2006.

2005. "Storm and Crisis: Government Assistance; Breakdowns Marked Path from Hurricane to Anarchy." September 11a. *www.nytimes.com*, accessed May 4, 2006.

2005. "Storm and Crisis: The Police; Duty Binds Officers Who Have Gone to Help After Storm." September 11b. *www.nytimes.com*, accessed May 4, 2006.

2005. "Storm and Crisis: Rumors; Authorities Struggling to Set Record Straight." September 12. *www.nytimes.com*, accessed May 4, 2006.

2005. "The Nation: Confidence Factor; Post-Katrina, Bricks and Mortals." September 18. *www.nytimes.com*, accessed May 4, 2006.

2005. "Storm and Crisis: Lawlessness; Fear Exceeded Crime's Reality in New Orleans." September 29. *www.nytimes.com*, accessed May 4, 2006.

Bibliography

2005. "Storm and Crisis: Law Enforcement; A Police Department Racked by Doubt and Accusations." September 30. *www.nytimes.com*, accessed May 4, 2006.

2005. "Angry Immigrants Embroil France in Wider Riots." November 5. *www.nytimes.com*, accessed, May 7, 2006.

2005. "Riots and Violence Spread from Paris to Other French Cities." November 6. *www.nytimes.com*, accessed May 7, 2006.

2005. "10 Officers Shot as Riots Worsen in French Cities." November 7. *www.nytimes.com*, accessed May 7, 2006.

2005. "Firestorm in France: The Police; Suburban Officers Criticized as Insensitive to Racism." November 8. *www.nytimes.com*, accessed May 7, 2006.

2005. "France Declares Emergency; Curfews to be Imposed." November 9. *www.nytimes.com*, accessed May 7, 2006.

2005. "The French Riots: A Political Scorecard." November 13. *www.nytimes.com*, accessed May 7, 2006.

2005. "What Britain Can Tell France about Rioters." November 20. *www.nytimes.com*, accessed May 7, 2006.

O'Donnell, Guilermo. 1993. "On the State, Democratization and Some Conceptual Problems: A Latin American View with Glances at Some Postcommunist Countries." *World Development* 21(August):1355–69.

1992. "Delegative Democracy?" The Helen Kellogg Institute for International Studies, University of Notre Dame 172, Working Paper.

Olzak, S. 1992. *The Dynamics of Ethnic Competition and Conflict*. Stanford, California: Stanford University Press.

1989. "Analysis of Events in Studies of Collective Action." *Annual Review of Sociology* 15:119–41.

Osa, Maryjane. 2003. "Networks of Opposition: Linking Organizations Through Activists in the Polish People's Republic." Pp. 77–104 in *Social Movements and Networks. Relational Approaches to Collective Action*, edited by Mario Diani and Doug McAdam. New York: Oxford University Press, 2003.

Otero, Daniel. 1997. *El Entorno. La Trama Intima del Aparato Duhaldista y sus Punteros*. Buenos Aires: Nuevohacer.

Oviedo, Luis. 2001. *Una Historia del Movimiento Piquetero*. Buenos Aires: Ediciones Rumbos.

Palermo, Vicente and Marcos Novaro. 1996. *Política y Poder en el Gobierno de Menem*. Buenos Aires: Grupo Editorial Norma.

Parenti, Christian. 2006. "The Big Easy Dies Hard." *The Nation*, September 26. *www.thenation.com*, accessed May 9, 2006.

Passy, Florence. 2003. "Social Networks Matter. But How?" Pp. 21–48 in *Social Movements and Networks: Relational Approaches to Collective Action*, edited by Mario Diani and Doug McAdam. New York: Oxford University Press.

Piven, Frances Fox and Richard A. Cloward. 1979. *Poor People's Movements: Why They Succeed, How They Fail*. New York: Vintage.

Prevot-Schapira, Marie. 1993. "La consolidación municipal en el Gran Buenos Aires: tensiones y ambiguedades." *Estudios Sociológicos* XI(33):25–47.

Prunier, Gerard. 1997. *The Rwanda Crisis: History of a Genocide*. New York: Columbia University Press.

Puex, Nathalie. 2003. "Las Formas de la Violencia en Tiempos de Crisis: Una Villa Miseria del Conurbano Bonaerense." Pp. 33–60 in *Heridas Urbanas. Violencia Delictiva y Transformaciones Sociales en los Noventa*, edited by Alejandro Isla and Daniel Miguez. Buenos Aires: Editorial de las Ciencias.

Ragin, Charles and Howard Becker, editors. 1992. *What Is a Case? Exploring the Foundations of Social Inquiry*. Cambridge: Cambridge University Press.

Rock, David. 2005. "Argentina: A Hundred and Fifty Years of Democratic Praxis." *Latin American Research Review* 40(2):221–34.

——— 1975. *Politics in Argentina: The Rise and Fall of Radicalism, 1890–1930*. Cambridge: Cambridge University Press.

Rodríguez Larreta, Fernando. 2000. "Descentralización de políticas sociales." Unpublished Manuscript. Buenos Aires: University of Buenos Aires.

Rofman, Alejandro. 2000. Destrucción De Las Economias Provinciales. *Le Monde Diplomatique*, August 6–7.

Roldán, Mary. 2002. *Blood and Fire: La Violencia in Antioquia, Colombia, 1946–1953*. Durham, North Carolina: Duke University Press.

Roniger, Luis. 1990. *Hierarchy and Trust in Modern Mexico and Brazil*. New York: Praeger.

Rose, Harold M. 1971. *The Black Ghetto: A Spatial Behavioral Perspective*. New York: McGraw-Hill.

Rosenfeld, Michael. 1997. "Celebration, Politics, Selective Looting and Riots: A Micro Level Study of the Bulls Riot of 1992 in Chicago." *Social Problems* 44(4):483–502.

Rosnow, Ralph. 1988. Rumor as Communication: A Contextualist Approach. *Journal of Communication* 38(1):12–28.

Rothen, Diana. 2000. *Global-Local Conditions of Possibility: The Case of Education Decentralization in Argentina*. Ph.D. Dissertation. Department of Education, Stanford University.

Rother, Larry. 2003. "Argentine Moves Against Police Corruption." *New York Times*, November 16.

Roy, Beth. 1994. *Some Trouble with Cows*. Berkeley: University of California Press.

Roy, Olivier, 2006. "The Nature of French Riots." *www.ssrc.org*, accessed May 6, 2006.

Rubins, Roxana and Horacio Cao. 2000. "Las Satrapías de Siempre." *Le Monde Diplomatique*, August 8–9.

Rudé, George. 1964. *The Crowd in History*. New York: John Wiley and Sons.

Rule, James. 1988. *Theories of Civil Violence*. Berkeley: University of California Press.

Sain, Marcelo. 2004. *Política, Policía y Delito. La red bonaerense*. Buenos Aires: Capital Intelectual.

Bibliography

2002. *Seguridad, Democracia y Reforma del Sistema Policial en la Argentina*. Buenos Aires: Fondo de Cultura Económica.

Salert, Barbara and John Sprague. 1980. *The Dynamics of Riots*. Ann Arbor: Inter-University Consortium for Political and Social Research.

Sanchez, Gonzalo and Donny Meertens. 2001. *Bandits, Peasants, and Politics: The Case of "La Violencia" in Colombia*. Austin: University of Texas Press.

Scheper-Hughes, Nancy. 1992. *Death Without Weeping: The Violence of Everyday Life in Brazil*. Berkeley: University of California Press.

Schmidt, Steffen W. 1974. "La Violencia Revisited: The Clientelist Bases of Political Bases in Colombia." *Journal of Latin American Studies* 6(1):97–111.

Schneider, Jane and Peter Schneider. 2003. *Reversible Destiny: Mafia, Antimafia, and the Struggle for Palermo*. Berkeley: University of California Press.

Schuster, Federico. 2002. "La Trama de la Crisis. Modos y Formas de Protesta Social a partir de los Acontecimientos de Diciembre de 2001," *Informes de Coyuntura* 3. Instituto Gino Germani, UBA.

Scott, James. 1977. "Patronage or Exploitation?" Pp. 67–94 in *Patrons and Clients in Mediterranean Societies*, edited by Ernest Gellner and John Waterbury. London: Duckworth.

Scott, James and Benedict J. Kerkvliet. 1977. "How Traditional Rural Patrons Lose Legitimacy: A Theory with Special Reference to Southeast Asia." Pp. 439–58 in *Friends, Followers, and Factions: A Reader in Political Clientelism*, edited by Laura Guasti, Carl Landé, James Scott, and Steffen Schmidt. Berkeley: University of California Press.

Scribano, Adrián. 1999. "Argentina "Cortada": Cortes de Ruta y Visibilidad Social en el Contexto del Ajuste." Pp. 45–72 in *Lucha Popular, Democracia, Neoliberalismo: Protesta Popular en América Latina en los Años del Ajuste*, edited by Margarita López Maya. Caracas, Venezuela: Nueva Sociedad.

Scribano, Adrián and Federico Schuster. 2001. Protesta Social en la Argentina de 2001: entre la normalidad y la ruptura. *OSAL* September.

Semán, Pablo. 2000. "El Pentecostalismo y la Religiosidad de los Sectores Populares." *Apuntes de Investigación* 5:35–58.

Serulnikov, Sergio. 1994. "When Looting Becomes a Right: Urban Poverty and Food Riots in Argentina." *Latin American Perspectives* 21(3):69–89.

Sewell, William. 2002. "Space in Contentious Politics." Pp. 51–88 in *Silence and Voice in the Study of Contentious Politics*, edited by Ronald Aminzade et al. New York: Cambridge University Press.

Shaheed, Farida. 1990. "The Pathan-Muhajir Conflicts, 1985–6: A National Perspective." Pp. 194–214 in *Mirrors of Violence. Communities, Riots and Survivors in South Asia*, edited by Veena Das. Oxford: Oxford University Press.

Silverstein, Paul and Chantal Tetreault. 2006. "Postcolonial Urban Apartheid." *www.ssrc.org*, accessed May 6, 2006.

Sitrin, Marina. 2005. *Horizontalidad. Voces de Poder Popular en Argentina*. Buenos Aires: Chilavert.

Smith, Neil. 2006. "There's No Such Thing as a Natural Disaster." *www.ssrc.org*, accessed March 16, 2006.

Snow, David, Daniel M. Cress, Liam Downey, and Andrew W. Jones. 1998. "Disrupting the 'Quotidian': Reconceptualizing the Relationship Between Breakdown and the Emergence of Collective Action." *Mobilization* 3(1): 1–22.

Snow, David, Calvin Morrill, and Leon Anderson. 2003. "Elaborating Analytic Ethnography: Linking Fieldwork and Theory." *Ethnography* June 4:181–200.

Solnit, Rebecca. 2005. "The Uses of Disaster." *Harper's Magazine*, September 9. *www.harpers.org*, accessed May 4, 2006.

Spillerman, Seymour. 1970. "The Causes of Racial Disturbance: A Comparison of Alternative Explanations." *American Sociological Review* 35(August):627–49.

Stark, Margaret Abudu, Walter Raine, Stephen Burbeck, and Keith Davison. 1974. "Some Empirical Patterns in a Riot Process." *American Sociological Review* 39(December):865–76.

Stein, Steve. 1980. *Populism in Perú: The Emergence of the Masses and the Politics of Social Control.* Madison: The University of Wisconsin Press.

Stillwaggon, Eileen. 1998. *Stunted Lives, Stagnant Economies: Poverty, Disease, and Underdevelopment.* New Brunswick, New Jersey: Rutgers University Press.

Stoller, Paul. 2004. *Stranger in the Village of the Sick: A Memoir of Cancer, Sorcery, and Healing.* New York: Beacon Press.

Svampa, Maristella and Sebastián Pereyra. 2003. *Entre la Ruta y el Barrio. La Experiencia de las Organizaciones Piqueteras.* Buenos Aires: Biblos.

Tarrow, Sidney. 1998. *Power in Movement: Social Movements and Contentious Politics.* New York: Cambridge University Press.

2005. *The New Transnational Activism.* New York: Cambridge University Press.

Taylor, Lynne. 1996. "Food Riots Revisited." *Journal of Social History* (Winter): 483–96.

Thompson, E. P. 1994. *Customs in Common.* New York: The New Press.

Tierney, Kathleen. 1994. "Property Damage and Violence: A Collective Behavior Analysis." Pp. 149–74 in *The Los Angeles Riots: Lessons for the Urban Future*, edited by Mark Baldassare. Boulder, Colorado: Westview Press.

Tilly, Charles. 2004. "Observations of Social Processes and Their Formal Representations." *Sociological Theory* 22(4):595–602.

2003. *The Politics of Collective Violence.* Cambridge, Massachusetts: Harvard University Press.

2000. "Spaces of Contention." *Mobilization* 5:135–60.

1992. "How to Detect, Describe, and Explain Repertoires of Contention." Center for the Study of Social Change, New School for Social Research, The Working Paper Series 150:6.

1986. *The Contentious French.* Cambridge, Massachusetts: Harvard University Press.

Bibliography

1978. *From Mobilization to Revolution*. Reading, Massachusetts: Addison Wesley.

1974. "Town and Country in Revolution." Pp. 154–78 in *Peasant Rebellion and Communist Revolution*, edited by John Wilson Lewis. Stanford, California: Stanford University Press.

Tilly, Charles, Louise Tilly, and Richard Tilly. 1975. *The Rebellious Century, 1830–1930*. Cambridge, Massachusetts: Harvard University Press.

Times Picayune (New Orleans). 2005. "Looting Suspects Stationed at Greyhound Terminal." September 9. *www.nola.com*, accessed May 8, 2006.

2005. "Makeshift Militia Patrols Algiers Neighborhood." September 8. *www.nola.com*, accessed May 8, 2006.

2005. "New Orleans Staggers to Its Feet for Next Step on Long Road." September 5. *www.nola.com*, accessed May 8, 2006.

2005. "Most Officers Working on Adrenaline, Little Else." September 4a. *www.nola.com*, accessed May 8, 2006.

2005. "New Orleans Staggers to Its Feet for Next Step on Long Road." September 4b. *www.nola.com*, accessed May 8, 2006.

2005. "Local Leaders Call Relief Efforts Too Little, Late: Violence, Looting Reported in East, West Jeff." September 2a. *www.nola.com*, accessed May 8, 2006.

2005. "Blanco Demands Thousands of Troops: Police Volunteers from Other States to Help Out." September 2b. *www.nola.com*, accessed May 8, 2006.

2005. "Supplies Running Scarce in Chaotic Jefferson." September 1a. *www.nola.com*, accessed May 8, 2006.

2005. "Forces Called in to Curb Widespread Looting." September 1b. *www.nola.com*, accessed May 8, 2006.

2005. "Looting on Tchoupitoulas Street." August 31. *www.nola.com*, accessed May 8, 2006.

Torres, Pablo. 2002. *Votos, Chapas y Fideos*. Buenos Aires: de la Campana.

Torresi, Leonardo. 2005. "El Coloso Olvidado." *www.clarin.com/diario/2005/05/22/sociedad/s-980980.htm*, accessed June 3, 2005.

Turner, Ralph and Lewis Killian. 1987. *Collective Behaviour*. Englewood Cliffs, New Jersey: Prentice-Hall.

United Nations Human Settlements Programme. 2003. *The Challenge of Slums. Global Report on Human Settlements*. London and Sterling, Virginia: Earthscan.

USA Today. 2005. "New Orleans Police May Have Participated in Looting." September 29. *www.usatoday.com*, accessed May 7, 2006.

Useem, Bert. 1985. Disorganization and the New Mexico Prison Riot of 1980. *American Sociological Review* 50:677–88.

1997. The State and Collective Disorders: The Los Angeles Riot/Protest of April, 1992. *Social Forces* 72(2):357–77.

1998. Breakdown Theories of Collective Action. *Annual Review of Sociology* 24:215–38.

Valentine, Daniel. 1996. *Charred Lullabies*. Princeton, New Jersey: Princeton University Press.

Vales, Laura. 2003a. "Plan y patota, receta Cariglino." *Página12Digital,* November 30, accessed March 13, 2006.

——— 2003b. "Desalojo de un asentamiento sin orden judicial, pero con punteros." *Página12Digital,* March 31, accessed March 17, 2005.

——— 2001. "Saqueos en Moreno." *Página12Digital,* December 20, accessed December 23, 2001.

Vanderwood, Paul. 1992. *Disorder and Progress: Bandits, Police, and Mexican Development*. Wilmington, Delaware: Scholarly Resources.

Varshney, Ashutosh. 2002. *Ethnic Conflict and Civic Life: Hindus and Muslims in India*. New Haven, Connecticut: Yale University Press.

Verbitsky, Horacio. 2002. "La Marca." *Página12Digital,* August 4, accessed March 1, 2005.

Villalón, Roberta. 2002. "Piquetes, Cacerolazos y Asambleas Vecinales: Social Protests in Argentina, 1993–2002." M.A. Thesis. University of Texas at Austin.

Villarreal, Andrés. 2002. "Political Competition and Violence in Mexico: Hierarchical Social Control in Local Patronage Structures." *American Sociological Review* 67(August):477–98.

Volkov, Vadim. 2002. *Violent Entrepreneurs: The Use of Force in the Making of Russian Capitalism*. Ithaca, New York: Cornell University Press.

Wacquant, Loïc. 2004. "Comment on Paul Farmer's An Anthropology of Structural Violence." *Current Anthropology* 45(3):322.

——— 2003. *Body and Soul*. Oxford: Oxford University Press.

——— 2002. "Scrutinizing the Street: Poverty, Morality, and the Pitfall of Urban Ethnography." *American Journal of Sociology* 107(6):1468–532.

——— 1993. "The Return of the Repressed. Urban Violence, 'Race,' and Dualization in Three Advanced Societies." Plenary address presented at the XVII Encontro Annual da ANPOCS, Caxambu, Brazil.

Wallman, Joel. 2000. "Common Sense about Violence: Why Research? Year 2000." Report of the Harry Frank Guggenheim Foundation.

Walton, John. 1989. "Debt, Protest, and the State in Latin America." Pp. 299–328 in *Power and Popular Protest: Latin American Social Movements*, edited by Susan Eckstein. Berkeley: University of California Press.

Walton, John and Charles Ragin. 1990. "Global and National Sources of Political Protest: Third World Responses to the Debt Crisis." *American Sociological Review* 55:876–90.

Walton, John and David Seddon. 1994. *Free Markets and Food Riots: The Politics of Global Adjustment*. Cambridge: Blackwell.

Walton, John and Jon Shefner. 1994. "Latin America: Popular Protest and the State." Pp. 97–134 in *Free Markets and Food Riots*, edited by John Walton and David Seddon. Cambridge: Blackwell.

Weber, Max. 1949. *The Methodology of the Social Sciences*. New York: Free Press.

Bibliography

Wilkinson, Steven. 2004. *Votes and Violence: Electoral Competition and Ethnic Riots in India*. Cambridge: Cambridge University Press.

Wohlenberg, Earnest H. 1982. "The 'Geography of Civility' Revisted: New York Blackout Looting, 1977." *Economic Geography* 58:29–44.

Wright, Angus and Wendy Wolford. 2003. *To Inherit the Earth: The Landless Movement and the Struggle for a New Brazil*. Oakland: Food First.

Yashar, Deborah. 1999. "Democracy, Indigenous Movements, and the Postliberal Challenge in Latin America." *World Politics* 51(1):76–104.

Young, Gerardo. 2002. "La Trama Política de los Saqueos." *Clarín Digital*, December 19.

Zhao, Dingxin. 2001. *The Power of Tiananmen: State-Society Relations and the 1989 Beijing Student Movement*. Chicago: University of Chicago Press.

Zussman, Robert. 2004. "People in Places." *Qualitative Sociology* 27/4:351–63.

Periodicals

Clarín, Crónica, Cronica-Chubut, El Ciudadano, El Liberal, El Litoral, El Sol, El Universal (Venezuela), *La Gaceta, La Mañana del Sur, La Nación, La Voz del Interior, Los Andes, Página12, Para Ud!*, and *Rio Negro*.

Index

Index

Tucumán, 73, 74, 80, 81, 90,
136, 137
Turner, Ralph, 15

Unidad Básica, 63, 64, 68, 93
Unidades Básicas, 59, 68,
114
United Nations Human
Settlements Programme,
111
Uruguay, 154
Useem, Bert, 15, 17, 20,
152
Uttar Pradesh, 87

Vales, Laura, 38, 91, 100, 127
validation, 27, 110, 122
Venezuela, 74, 153, 154
Villalón, Roberta, 79

Volkov, Vadim, 19
Votes and Violence, 18

Wacquant, Loïc, 7, 8, 9, 27
Walton, John, 16
Weber, Max, 25
West, Mariano, 109
Whan Cai So, 143
Wilkinson, Steven, 18, 19, 33, 87,
123
Wohlenberg, Earnest H., 15
Wohlstein, Ronald, 15, 94
World Bank, 61

Yashar, Deborah, 157
Young, Dingxin, 22, 95, 129

Zero Deficit Law, 99
Zussman, Robert, 24